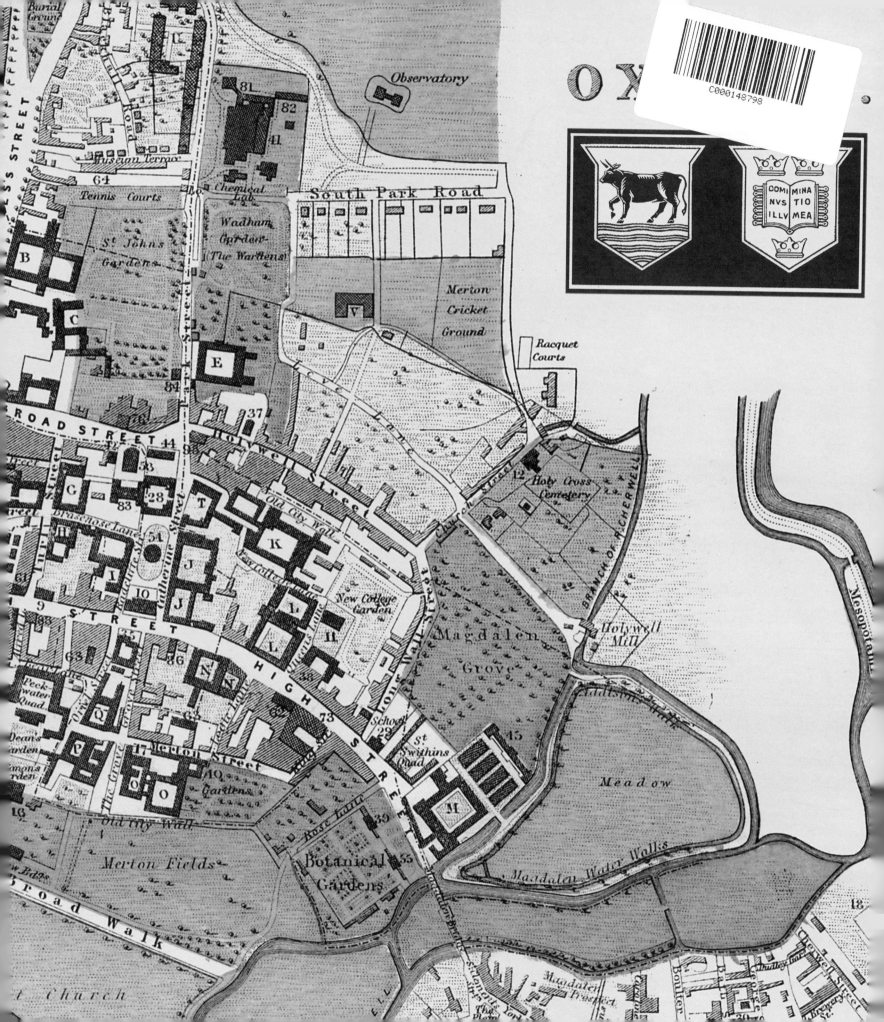

O X

Burial Ground

LESS STREET

Observatory

81
82
41

Museum Terrace
64

Tennis Courts

Chemical Lab.

Wadham Garden
(The Wardens)

South Park Road

St Johns Gardens

B

V

Merton Cricket Ground

C

Racquet Courts

E

84

DOMI MINA
NVS TIO
ILLV MEA

ROAD STREET

176

37

Holwell Street

BRANCH OF CHERWELL

Mesopotamia

44
98

53

Holy Cross Cemetery

G

83

28

12

Brasenose Lane

Catherine Street

54

Old City Wall

T

K

New College Garden

H

J

J

61

10

Holywell Mill

9

L

L

Magdalen Grove

STREET

63

HIGH

L

Holywell Mill

86

N

N

Peckwater Quad

Addison Walk

Q

School
29

45

Dean's Garden

P

17

Merton Street

St Swithins Quad

Meadow

O

O

Gardens

16

Old City Wall

39

M

Magdalen Water Walks

Merton Fields

Rose Lane

Botanical Gardens

55

18

Broad Walk

Church

Magdalen Prospect

Boulter

OXFORD

· MEMORIES OF TIMES PAST ·

· 60 PAINTINGS BY JOHN FULLEYLOVE ·

INTRODUCTION BY TIM HEALEY
TEXT BY SU BOX AND COLIN INMAN

A NOTE TO THE READER

In order to keep the pages of the book as uncluttered as possible,
all sources, notes and captions relating to illustrations other than
the main paintings have been grouped at the end of the book,
and will be found on pages 137–9.

The endpaper maps of Oxford (front) and Oxfordshire (back)
are from the *Atlas of the British Isles* published in 1902 by G.W. Bacon.

First published in the UK in 2007 by Worth Press Ltd, Cambridge, United Kingdom.

Tim Healey, Su Box and Colin Inman have asserted their rights
under the Copyright and Patents Act 1988 to be identified as the authors of the book

Copyright © 2007 Worth Press Ltd
Concept, design and layout © 2007 Bookcraft Ltd

All reasonable efforts have been made to trace original copyright holders

Project manager   John Button
Design manager   Lucy Guenot

Set in Centaur and Gill Sans by Bookcraft Ltd, Stroud, Gloucestershire
Printed in Malaysia by Imago

A Memories of Times Past title
www.memoriesoftimespast.com

ISBN 978 1 903025 52 9

⁞⁞⁞ CONTENTS

OXFORD

ANDREW LANG

DOMI
NVS
ILLV
MINA
TIO
MEA

OXFORD.

From Original
Water = =
Colour = =
Paintings

By A. R. Quinton.

COLLEGE BARGES, FOLLY BRIDGE

OXFORD

Pictured by Ernest Haslehust
Described by F. D. Ha

OXFORD 1903

TIM HEALEY

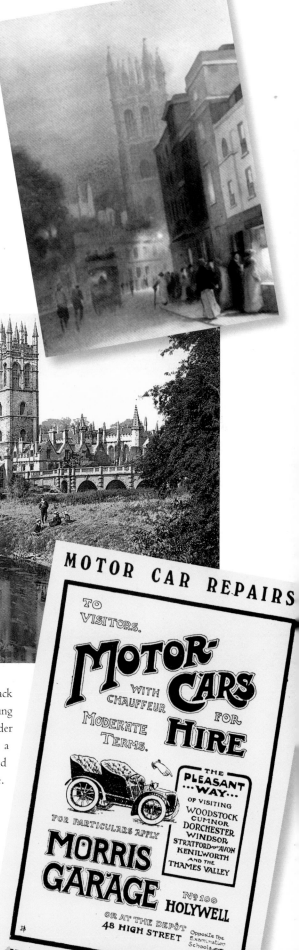

John Fulleylove's Oxford is a city of the golden age. Often lit by late afternoon sunshine, with the shadows of noble trees and spires lengthening across college lawns, the scenes exude a monumental quietness, the ambience of a sacred city. Black-gowned scholars move at an unhurried pace through lanes and gardens, dwarfed by the venerable architecture.

Here and there the artist's brush may sketch a diminutive group of Edwardian ladies in straw hats and long skirts; in a corner of Broad Street we discern a bicycle. Otherwise very little of the twentieth-century world disturbs Fulleylove's university city. Its mystique was already timeless. "Oxford!" wrote author and caricaturist Max Beerbohm; "The very sight of the word printed, or sound of it spoken, is fraught for me with the most actual magic."

You would not guess from these quiet images that in 1903 traffic jams were already causing problems in Oxford streets. Magdalen Bridge had recently been widened to accommodate the numbers of horse-drawn trams which thronged the city, brashly advertising

10,084. P. Z. - OXFORD. MAGDALEN TOWER.

Margett's Hats, Van Houten's Cocoa and Nixey's Black Lead. Oxford had entered the motoring age. A young entrepreneur named William Morris, future founder of Morris Motors, had already set himself up in a garage on Longwall Street where he sold, repaired and hired out motor vehicles to a growing clientele.

Magdalen Tower, painted by Yoshio Markino in 1905 and reproduced in Hugh de Sélincourt's *Oxford from Within* (top); Magdalen Tower, a late 1890s photochrome (above); an advertisement from Davis's *Short Guide to Oxford*, 1906 (right)

THE ISIS AND BARGES

Nov 18 1902

MOTOR CAR REPAIRS

TO VISITORS.

MOTOR-CARS

WITH CHAUFFEUR

FOR

MODERATE TERMS.

HIRE

THE PLEASANT ...WAY...

OF VISITING

WOODSTOCK
CUMNOR
DORCHESTER
WINDSOR
STRATFORD-on-AVON
KENILWORTH
AND THE
THAMES VALLEY

FOR PARTICULARS APPLY

MORRIS GARAGE

Nº 100 HOLYWELL

OR AT THE DEPÔT
48 HIGH STREET

Opposite the Examination Schools.

The de Dion–Bouton Tonneau, a top-of-the-range touring car from a 1907 French postcard.

Suffragettes demonstrating in 1913, from the Odhams pictorial souvenir *The Pageant of the Century*.

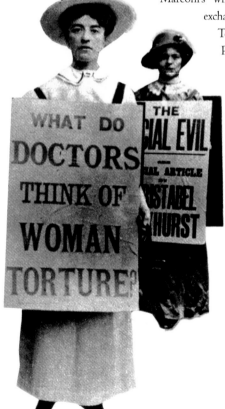

Popular models included runabouts like the Daimler and De Dion, open to the weather so that male drivers sought protection in big leather topcoats and women went thickly veiled under their hats. A recently-enacted Act of Parliament required owners to register their vehicle for 20 shillings per year, and to acquire a driving license costing 5 shillings.

In Oxford, as elsewhere, drivers now had to observe a speed limit of 20 mph, with heavy fines for speeding and reckless driving. Local motoring enthusiasts nonetheless had something to celebrate that year. The inaugural event of the Oxford Motor Club was held on 1 March 1903. It opened with a "Reliability Trial" which started from the now vanished Clarendon Hotel in Cornmarket Street, participants testing their vehicles on the 15-mile route to Wallingford.

The world was shrinking. In 1903 a regular news service opened between London and New York, using Marconi's wireless. Oxford had two telephone exchanges, one owned by the National Telephone Company, the other by the Post Office Trunk Exchange. Besides individual home owners, telephone subscribers included the colleges, the big hotels, and the fire and police stations.

In 1903 Emily Pankhurst formed the Women's Social and Political Union to secure votes for women. Under the slogan "Deeds not Words", Mrs Pankhurst spoke at Oxford's Victorian Town Hall, which became a venue for rowdy meetings by suffragettes and anti-suffragists alike. Throughout the land, a decade of mass rallies and protests climaxed in a furore in 1913

when women activists mounted a campaign of letter-box fires. Oxford was not immune. Nine pillar boxes in the city were damaged with green fluid and printer's ink, and a hundred letters were destroyed. At the ancient heart of the city, a pillar box at Carfax was daubed in green paint "Down with Lloyd George!!!", and when it was opened a letter bomb – constructed from fragments of glass, cotton wool and an inflammable substance – burst into flames.

Yet Fulleylove's Oxford gives no premonition of such alarms. His is "that sweet City with her dreaming spires" fêted by the poet Matthew Arnold. The fabric of the city which upholsters his illustrations has lost none of its allure today. Historic Oxford continues to furnish pedigree backdrops for film and television – Brideshead Revisited, Inspector Morse, the Harry Potter films and countless others.

"ALL'S AS IT WAS, ALL'S AS IT WILL BE"
Paintings may catch the beauty of Oxford, but not its voice. Always idiosyncratic, the great University shaped futures in offbeat ways. Leonard Woolley, celebrated as excavator of the great city of Ur in Iraq, took his degree in 1903. He was at New College, and was invited at the end of his term to the lodgings of the warden, the eccentric William Spooner. Asked by the warden what he proposed to do with his life, Woolley replied that he intended to be a schoolmaster. "Oh, yes; a schoolmaster, really; well, Mr Woolley, I have decided that you shall be an archaeologist." There was no more to be said.

Between 1900 and the outbreak of the Great War, other important names of the future were pursuing their studies here. T.E. Lawrence, a local boy from Oxford High School, read history at Jesus College, taking his degree in 1910. As an undergraduate, the youth who would win fame as "Lawrence of Arabia" already showed a taste for adventure. Checking out tales of old underground tunnels in Oxford, he discovered the existence of a hidden Trill Mill stream with one end at the mouth of a sewer at Hythe Bridge. With a canoe and cycle lamp he ventured into the darkness of the uncharted sewer, propelling himself by the damp walls, with no room to turn back. In less than twenty minutes he emerged at Folly Bridge. The trip subsequently became popular among fellow students, until it was stopped by the authorities.

J.R.R. Tolkien, future author of *The Lord of the Rings*, was reading English at Exeter College at the time when the Great War broke out. C.S. Lewis was at University College. With other Oxford academics they went on to found the famous discussion group, known as the Inklings, who would stimulate new literary interest in fantasy fiction. They also created new mystiques of Oxford through their meetings in Lewis's college rooms at Magdalen and their gatherings at the Eagle and Child – a pub they called the "Bird and Baby".

A hundred years ago, American tourists with Baedeker guides and push-button Kodak cameras were already coming to Oxford in large numbers. They often described, in wonder and alarm, how England's brightest prospects were still housed at Oxford in dilapidated medieval buildings, without fire escapes, ventilation, sanitation or up-to-date cooking facilities. As late as 1922 the Canadian writer Stephen Leacock wrote of Oxford college accommodation: "The buildings at Brasenose College have not been renewed since the year 1525. In New College and Magdalen the students are still housed in the old buildings erected in the sixteenth century. At Christ Church I was shown a kitchen which had been built at the expense of Cardinal Wolsey in 1527. Incredible though it may seem, they have no other place to cook in than this and are compelled to use it to-day. I could not help contrasting it with the cosy little boarding-houses where I used to eat when I was a student at Chicago, or the charming little basement dining-rooms of the students' boarding houses in Toronto."

Yet modern life had by no means bypassed the city. By 1910 the Randolph Hotel was offering handsome suites supplied with electricity, as well as "an American elevator" and a garage for cars. On Cornmarket Street, visitors could take refreshment at the Clarendon Hotel, or at Buol's which from 1902 to 1919 advertised "the very finest dining hotel and restaurant in the city". It had a coffee and tea saloon as well as a second-floor dining room, and another below where guests could enjoy the waltz, still the favoured dance of the day.

The more ancient buildings, however, set the tone of the city. For Max Beerbohm, writing in 1911, Oxford's timeless quality was evoked by the daily tolling of the immense Christ Church bell,

Advertisements from *Alden's Oxford Guide*, 1902; "Cleaning" from *Woman at Home* Christmas colour supplement 1910.

3

Mitre Hotel, a 1901 postcard (top);
advertisement from *Alden's Oxford Guide*, 1902
(bottom).

Great Tom. "Stroke by stroke the great familiar monody of that incomparable curfew rose and fell … 'All's as it was, all's as it will be,' says Great Tom."

All was especially well at The Mitre, perhaps the most seductive of the city's old coaching inns. Here guests were treated to lobster cutlets, devilled sweetbreads, neck of venison and marrow bones (a speciality of the house), refreshing themselves with hock, claret and champagne. The inn was off-limits to undergraduates, but the wealthier nonetheless feasted here surreptitiously, keeping watch on the door for the university police – the Proctors and Bulldogs.

Glimpsed in Fulleylove's view of the High Street, the inn was a proverb as much for its antiquated appearance as for its gastronomic delights. Visiting The Mitre around the turn of the century, a Harvard man wrote in his university magazine of its aged beams and low-ceilinged rooms, the courtyard with its gnarled trees growing from the cracked flagging. The legendary cuisine was prepared in a curious old kitchen with ancient spits and cooking arrangements. "You are not surprised when they tell you, as they are proud of doing, that this inn was established in the year 1400. As for the rooms upstairs, there is such a maze of passage-ways and old chambers that one almost needs a guide-book to find his way about the house."

TOWN AND GOWN

Dating from the twelfth century, Oxford University is one of the oldest in Europe. Over the centuries it evolved as a federation of individual colleges scattered around the town, rather than as a single campus. Colleges were built much like monasteries, each with its own dining hall, quadrangles, chapel and library. Colleges owned their own premises, and in many cases held valuable lands and assets both in Oxford and further afield. The teaching staff, known as Fellows, governed their own demesnes; and in 1903 the University still possessed age-old privileges over the townsfolk of Oxford.

From public schools throughout the land, the offspring of wealthy Edwardian families came to sojourn in the rich seclusion of Oxford, prior to taking up key posts in national life as statesmen, bishops, governors, judges, poets laureate and civil servants. Their choice of college would help stamp their character. Christ Church boasted a centuries-old reputation as the chief resort of English aristocracy. Balliol, meanwhile, had acquired a name both for intellectual prowess and hospitality to non-white and non-aristocratic students. Brasenose College was famed for sport, and its hearty tradition was exemplified by all-rounder Arnold Strode-Jackson, who rowed, played football, and three times won the mile race for Oxford against Cambridge. His apotheosis came at Stockholm in 1912 when he won the Olympic gold medal for the 1500 metres – while still an undergraduate.

In 1907 a writer in the *National Review* identified subtler traits. Trinity College, was "the proud possessor of a certain element of muscular Christianity", while the average New College man was "not intolerant of learning, but he is possibly more prone to admire it in others than to seek it for himself".

The great outlet for college rivalries was sport. In Bumping Races on the river, rowing crews sought to catch and knock the boat ahead. During summer events known as "Eights and Torpids", crews were organised

in divisions and the overall winner earned the title "Head of the River". A celebratory Bump Supper was given by the college when its oarsmen won, and bonfires were fed with whatever came to hand. Richard Gunstone was for decades a steward at Magdalen College before his retirement in 1914, when he told the *Daily Chronicle* that students were not so reckless as they used to be. "Bump suppers are very subdued affairs; they used to burn as much as £50 of college property, but they don't now."

Note the nostalgic regret. College servants were a largely conservative class, infinitely tolerant of their binge-drinking lordlings – they were less comfortable with the new breed of students who drank cocoa in their rooms, reading socialist tracts. In Oxford's student argot, the legendary Gunstone was affectionately known as "Gunner" in the same way that the Bulldogs were "Bullers". The idiom changed the ends of all significant words to "–er". A bemused Worcester College freshman recorded an example in his diary for 1911: "After Toggers brekker went to divers leccer, then to eat at the Ugger." (After Torpids breakfast I went to a Divinity lecture then ate at the Oxford Union.)

Among college servants, the "scouts" were especially important figures to the Edwardian undergraduate, for they were mature men, and wise in college ways. The scout was the student's personal servant, who in the morning made his coal fire and brought breakfast up to his rooms. Traditionally scouts had also trimmed the oil lamps, but by 1905 all colleges except Keble

had electric lighting. They did not, however, have hot water on tap. Scouts took care of each "staircase", for it was up and down stairs, rather than along corridors, that most rooms were arranged. In the evening they brought hot water up from the pantry to a hip bath by the fire, then carried the tepid water down afterwards.

To knit together the self-governing colleges, the University had its own officers, among whom the Chancellor was chief. He presided over the University ceremonial which included the Encaenia, the climax of the academic year, when degrees were conferred at the Sheldonian Theatre.

The University, under its Chancellor, had extensive powers over the city. Its grip over Oxford was sealed as early as 1355 when their difficult relations erupted in the worst town versus gown rioting that the city has ever known. On 10 February, St Scholastica's Day, pitched battles between students and citizens led to sixty-three scholars being slain. A subsequent enquiry found the townsmen to blame, and the University afterwards won new authority in civic affairs, including policing.

Oxford Eights, a 1903 Frith postcard (top left); Oxford Eights again, from a 1905 Frith pictorial folding souvenir (top right); the Oxford boat crew of 1906, from a "real photograph" postcard (above).

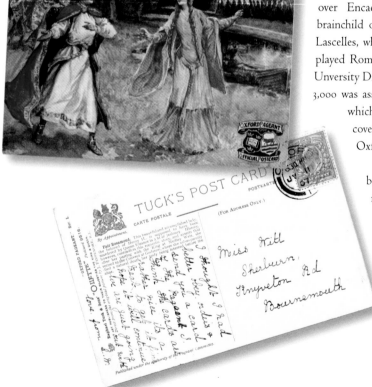

The Official Souvenir of the 1907 Oxford Historical Pageant, and a selection of Tuck's colour postcards issued to commemorate the event.

Oxford has a long memory. In Edwardian times the University still possessed remarkable privileges over the city, and the two bodies were at loggerheads over many issues. But in June 1907 age-old differences were buried as they co-operated on the committee of an Oxford Historical Pageant. This gigantic and colourful new enterprise was staged over Encaenia Week and was the brainchild of the theatre-loving Frank Lascelles, who as an undergraduate had played Romeo at OUDS (the Oxford Unversity Dramatic Society). A team of 3,000 was assembled to stage the event, which depicted sixteen scenes covering a thousand years of Oxford history.

The spectacle was staged before a grandstand by the river, with royal barges and Viking warships, choirs of Franciscan monks, a platform for the orchestra and a bridge that costumed horsemen could gallop on. The University, at first doubtful about the spectacle, became seized by its romance. Dons reportedly queued up to swagger on as Roger Bacon, Henry VIII or the Earl of Leicester, while scriptwriters included such eminent Oxford men as the poet Robert Bridges.

The ordinary people of Oxford were involved too. Mr Wiblin, a local butcher, was among the trumpeters, and his programme for the event was afterwards found in his bureau drawer. Pencilled notes included the instruction "send piccolo player up on to the roof where the nymphs need help". The grand finale called for the whole Pageant to stream off over the bridge to a favourite hymn: Mr Wiblin's scribbles include an urgent note to "keep going with O, God our Help".

Chancellor Curzon, with university officials in their robes, conducted some distinguished guests to the viewing stand. Rudyard Kipling was there, as was Mark Twain, in Oxford for the week to be awarded his doctor's degree at the Encaenia. Inevitably there was some rain on the day, but all seats were covered and the Pageant was counted a triumph. "It was beyond anything I had imagined," Mark Twain told the *New York Times*. "I never meant to journey over any sea again except at my own funeral, but I would cross the Atlantic twice to see it."

TRADITION AND INNOVATION

The Pageant, as such events always do, skimmed over the seamier side of Oxford's history. It is doubtful whether John Fulleylove knew that his Grove Street, with its picturesque half-timbered buildings, first appears in the city records of the early Middle Ages as a place where prostitutes conducted their business. Making more legitimate contact with the opposite sex had never been an easy matter for Oxford scholars. For long centuries the University had been an all-male world where students were exclusively young men, and their tutors forbidden to marry. Except for occasional visits from mothers and sisters, all were bereft of female company while in college.

Things changed only late in the Victorian era. From 1877 the celibacy rule for college fellows was relaxed and senior members were permitted to marry. North Oxford, already expanding, experienced an intensified boom in the building of family houses. Many of the large red-brick Victorian mansions, with their generous, leafy gardens, were erected especially to accommodate the flood of newly uxorious Dons.

The first women's colleges appeared soon afterwards: Lady Margaret Hall, Somerville College, St Hugh's and St Hilda's. Early alumni included archaeologist and explorer Gertrude Bell, who studied at Lady Margaret Hall and was the first woman to attain first class in modern history. Mystery writer Dorothy L. Sayers read modern languages at Somerville and took her degree in 1915, the same year as Tolkien. Neither woman in her day, however, was a full member of the University. Even in this progressive time, female undergraduates had no official status. They might attend University lectures, sit examinations and have their results recorded, but it was not until 1920 that women were granted degrees from Oxford.

Diligent and carefully chaperoned, the new women students provoked no crisis of promiscuity. They came to learn, not to flirt. This is exemplified in Max Beerbohm's 1911 satire of Edwardian Oxford, *Zuleika Dobson*. The eponymous heroine is not a woman

Dorothy L. Sayers in 1916 (left); Gertrude Bell in Iraq, 1913 (right); William Spooner, in a Spy *Vanity Fair* cartoon of 1898 (below).

undergraduate, but the glamorous visiting relation of a college warden. Zuleika provokes such desperate desire that the entire student body drowns itself in the river for love of her.

For all the new features of University life, Edwardian Oxford still clung to its roots in tradition. Cloistered in venerable colleges with their ancient chapels and oak-panelled libraries, enjoying epic dinners and vintage port, the Dons remained a breed apart. Seclusion from outside life fostered eccentricity even among such likeable, conscientious souls as William Spooner, mentioned previously. He famously gave his name to the English usage "spoonerism", referring to the accidental transposition of the opening sounds of words, as in "fighting liars" instead of "lighting fires". But his strangeness had greater comic sweep, as in:

"Do come to dinner tonight to meet our new Fellow, Casson."

"But Warden, I am Casson."

"Never mind, come all the same."

and

"In the sermon I have just preached, whenever I said Aristotle I meant St Paul."

Perceiving the old guard to be an already vanishing tribe, J.R. Green wrote in his *Oxford Studies* of 1901 that "They were not as other men are. They had in fact a deep, quiet contempt for other men. Oxford was their world, and beyond Oxford lay only waste wide regions of shallowness and inaccuracy. They were often men of keen humour, of humour keen enough at any rate to see and to mock at the mere pretences of "the world of progress" around them. Their delight was to take a "progressive idea" and to roast it over the common-room fire."

In Victorian times, one of those progressive ideas had been that Oxford should have a railway station. The University blocked the idea for years on the grounds that a lower class inundation would corrupt student morals. Even when the Great Western Railway at last gained permission to reach Oxford, the University authorities were granted free access to every station, ticket office and platform. Importantly, they had powers to stop students from travelling even if they had paid their fare. Junior members could be carried to some stations and not to others (Ascot, site of the celebrated racecourse, was one of those proscribed).

Oxford Station in 1900, a "real photograph" postcard.

By Edwardian times the railway had become a fixture of Oxford life, and visitors arriving at the station were met by horse-drawn omnibuses which carried them to the main hotels. A new debate opened up about public transport when, in 1905, the city authorities pressed for electric trams to replace horse-drawn vehicles. The University was appalled by the prospect of overhead power lines in The High and they never appeared on the scene. Motor buses offered an alternative on which the University was scarcely more keen. It would take a bold stroke by the car manufacturer, William Morris, to resolve the dispute.

THE BULLDOGS AND THE BOOM

The University's power over civic life was also evidenced by its disciplinary officers, the Proctors. They had their own private police force of constables, nick-named Bulldogs, who enjoyed the same powers as regular police within four miles of any university building. Every night in Edwardian Oxford, bowler-hatted Bulldogs patrolled the city streets, routinely seeking out any undergraduate who might be there without cap and gown. They also entered inns and hotels, which were prohibited to students, looking for any who might be roistering on the premises. If apprehended, victims were required to present themselves to the Proctors the next day, to face fines – and worse penalties for the graver offences.

The Proctors, with their Bulldogs, were a detective force, keeping eyes and ears open at all times for imminent escapades. Punishments depended very much on the character of the Proctors officiating. *Our Memories: Shadows of Old Oxford* records the case of a ball that was scheduled for a village near Oxford. Six undergraduates were rumoured to be going. This became known to the Proctors, who with Bulldogs and marshals got there first and surrounded the house at every door. They searched the premises, arrested five and took their names. The sixth could not be found, though his identity was discovered and he was summoned to the Proctors a few days later.

There, before he could attempt an alibi, he was told that his means of deception was already known; he had emulated a sofa. "When the confusion began, you threw yourself on your hands and knees on the floor; three of the female dancers sat upon your back, and spreading out their dresses effectually concealed you. You must be aware that you were guilty of a serious breach of discipline, but you have made no remark on my statement, and the mode of your escape was so ingenious that I am reluctant to punish you, and therefore wish you good morning."

The powers of the Proctors to patrol hotels and raid private houses became ever more anomalous as Oxford expanded. There was a huge building boom during the late Victorian and Edwardian periods. Red brick terraces sprawled out to north, south, east and west of the centre, and new manufacturing concerns sprang up, employing thousands of working men and women with no attachment to the University. In Edwardian times, Lucy's Eagle Ironworks was thriving in Jericho, Oxford's first working-class suburb. Labourers' dwellings had been growing round the premises on Walton Well Road ever since 1825, when a local ironmonger set up a works by the Oxford Canal. This network of waterways could bring coal, iron ore and limestone, while carrying his manufactures to their markets. Cast iron for pipes, lamp posts and manhole covers was a speciality, as was ornamental ironwork for gates and balconies.

Nearby, in Walton Street, a new Oxford University Press building was flourishing. From here tens of thousands of Bibles, school books and dictionaries streamed out across the world. The massive, authoritative *Oxford English Dictionary* appeared, though it did so with elephantine slowness. It took six years, from 1873 to 1879, to produce the first volume, A–Ant, and the work was not completed until 1928.

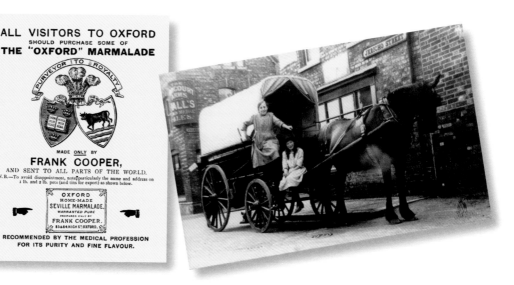

One local outlet for Oxford's burgeoning publishing industry was Blackwell's Bookshop, which in 1879 opened at 50 Broad Street in a tiny room just twelve feet square. It quickly grew to incorporate the upstairs, cellar and neighbouring shops, and is now one of the world's largest bookshops with more than 200,000 titles in stock. Blackwell's developed its own publishing firm too, through which J.R.R. Tolkien's first poem, "Goblin's Feet", was issued in 1915.

Other businesses were expanding at such a rate that they also had to move further out. Frank Cooper's Oxford Marmalade was a case in point. In 1874, from his shop at 84 High Street, a grocer named Frank Cooper began selling marmalade in earthenware jars. Made to an old family recipe by his wife Sarah Jane, it became so popular that in 1900 Frank Cooper Ltd opened more substantial works in Park End Street, close to the railway station. In the Age of Empire, Cooper's Oxford Marmalade became a worldwide brand; a jar of it went with Captain Scott on his ill-fated race to the South Pole to be found, many years after his death in 1912, buried in the ice.

Expansion was going on even underground. The old Bodleian Library had, by 1900, acquired such a volume of books that new storage space was needed for them. At the time that Fulleylove was painting Oxford, miles

Advertisement from *Alden's Oxford Guide*, 1902 (left); Jericho Street in 1900, a "real photograph" postcard (right); Broad Street at night painted by Yoshio Markino from *Oxford From Within*, 1905 (below).

Oxford Morris Garage in 1912, from Odham's *Pageant of the Century* (left); Martyrs' Memorial and St Giles, from Ernest Haslehurst's *Oxford* (right).

of underground tunnels were being dug for shelving. Today the Bodleian contains nine million publications on 176 km of shelving.

A new age of mass entertainment was signalled when The Electric Theatre, Oxford's first cinema, opened in November 1910. And the city's industrial apotheosis culminated in the same year, when William Morris conceived the manufacture of a cheap, reliable motor car for the middle classes. Production of the Morris-Oxford Light Car began in his Longwall Street works in 1912. The grey, leather-upholstered two-seater proved so successful that Morris sought larger premises at Temple Cowley, east of the city centre.

It was Morris who dramatically broke the deadlock between town and gown on the vexed question of public transport. One night in November 1913 he brought a dozen motor buses up from London – and the Oxford Motor Omnibus Company was born. The car manufacturer was becoming a major force in the life of the city; by the end of the following year, Morris Motors had sold 1,300 motor vehicles. Morris himself would soon become Viscount Nuffield, and found Nuffield College for post-graduate studies.

THE NEW OXFORD

These changes were bound to affect the character of what had been a sleepy market town servicing the University. Perhaps understandably, industrial Oxford does not feature in Fulleylove's illustrations, but nor do a wealth of new landmarks built in Victorian Gothic style. One was the Martyr's Memorial on St Giles, another the University Museum, an outlandish affair which included a Chemistry Laboratory modelled on the medieval Abbot's Kitchen at Glastonbury. Even Alfred Tennyson, who favoured medieval themes in his poetry, had balked at the University Museum – the design, he wrote, was "perfectly indecent". Looming large over Oxford's Edwardian skyline, yet another Victorian colossus was brick-built Keble College, erected to challenge the University's aristocratic exclusiveness, open to less affluent students and promoting a strong Christian ethos.

Between 1876 and 1914, no architect was more prolific than Thomas Graham Jackson. His buildings included the new Examination Schools, the chapel at Balliol, much of Hertford College, the Radcliffe

Science Library, two High Schools (one for boys and one for girls), and numerous restorations.

"Oxford Jackson", as he has been dubbed, drew on many past architectural styles; his Bridge of Sighs over New College Lane, for example, was modelled on the Rialto in Venice. He also ornamented his buildings with profuse carvings from sketches made during his extensive travels. Posterity was not kind to him, and following his death he was either forgotten or reviled as (in Peter Levi's words) "the only really preposterous architect". But taste may yet change again. The mysterious "Green Man" image – a leafy mask or human face disgorging foliage – was one of Jackson's favourite motifs. Medieval in origin and suggestive of human oneness with the earth, it appeals to twenty-first century environmentalists. Many of the Green Men seen among Oxford's gargoyles and grotesques are in fact the work of Victorian and Edwardian restorers – especially of Oxford Jackson.

Oxford's physical transformation was matched by a reforming spirit within the colleges themselves. Left-wing dons supported the foundation of Ruskin College, an institution providing residential education for working men with the hope of schooling future leaders of the Labour Movement. Finding a permanent home on Walton Street in 1903, it had strong links with trade unions and cooperative societies.

The agents of change in Oxford were not only free-thinking liberals and socialists. Cecil Rhodes had made a fortune in southern Africa and was a passionate advocate of the British Empire. He bequeathed huge sums to found scholarships for students to come to Oxford from throughout the English-speaking world, none being disqualified on grounds of race or religion. The first Rhodes Scholars arrived in Oxford in 1903, and to secluded colleges languishing in the Thames Valley they soon brought the accents of the United States, Canada, South and East Africa, Australia, India, Malaysia and the Caribbean.

People spoke of a New Oxford, looking to the future. Yet centuries of tradition still impressed their character on the University, and there is something almost elegiac in John Fulleylove's vision of its buildings bathed in sunshine. Before long, the nation would be set on course for a catastrophic war in which 2,700 Oxford men were to die. In every college memorials would go up to the budding politicians and sportsmen, lawyers and poets who fell in the mud of the Somme and the Marne. The artist gives no hint of coming conflict, but the shadows are lengthening over his oasis of ancient peace.

JOHN FULLEYLOVE
1844–1908

COLIN INMAN

John Fulleylove was born on 18 August 1844 in Leicester and baptised at St George's, Leicester, on 4 September the same year. Most published sources, including the *Dictionary of National Biography*, give his birth wrongly as either 1845 or 1846. He was the son of John Fulleylove, a carriage maker, who had built the first carriages designed by Joseph Hansom, and his wife Elizabeth, formerly Preston. He had four older siblings: Thomas (16 in 1851), coach painter; Maria (14), warehouse girl; William (12), errand boy; and Keturah (10), none of these occupations suggesting that the family was especially well off.

John was educated at the private school of Dr Highton and at the age of 16 was articled to Flint, Shenton and Baker, a Leicester firm of architects. Soon afterwards he began to study painting, receiving some tuition from Harry Ward, a local drawing master. His earliest drawings were of Leicester and its surrounds. He decided to take up art professionally, his first works being exhibited in London in 1871. He began to travel widely to find subjects to paint, touring Italy in 1875 and again in 1880. The summer of 1878 he spent sketching at Old Tabley Hall, that of 1879 at Hampton Court and of 1882 at Versailles.

In 1878 he married Elizabeth Sarah Elgood, daughter of Samuel Elgood of Leicester (and sister of the artist George S. Elgood, who also illustrated books for A&C Black, and was well known as a painter of gardens). They had a son and two daughters, one of whom, Joan (1886–1947), became a stained glass artist. The 1881 census finds the couple living with his parents at 24 Regent Street, Leicester; on other occasions, however, Fulleylove and his family seem to have been remarkably successful in evading census scrutiny.

Part of a Bastion of Old London with The Clock Tower of The White Tower, from *The Tower of London*, 1916 (top); Edinburgh from the Castle, from *Edinburgh*, 1920 (bottom).

Fulleylove became an associate of the Royal Institute of Painters in Water-Colours in 1878 and a member in 1879. In 1883 he moved with his family to London, living first in Mecklenburgh Square, then in Great Russell Street and finally at 21 Church Row, Hampstead, which remained his home until his death. His studio was at 1 Langham Chambers in Portland Place.

He held a number of exhibitions at the Fine Arts Society galleries in Bond Street, including views of Oxford in 1888, Cambridge in 1890 and Versailles in 1894. In 1895 he visited Greece with his friends Alfred Higgins and Somers Clarke, a trip which resulted in more than 100 watercolours and pencil drawings which were displayed at the Fine Arts Society in 1896 in an exhibition called *Greek Landscape and Architecture*. These are regarded as the peak of his achievement. Another exhibition in 1902 showed paintings of the Holy Land; these were the illustrations used in A&C Black's *The Holy Land*, which was published the same year.

Another exhibition of Oxford paintings at the Fine Arts Society in 1899, which included paintings later used in A&C Black's *Oxford*, was welcomed by *The Times* critic: "… when the painter is so sympathetic as Mr Fulleylove it is no wonder that he goes painting the beautiful city. This time, instead of water-colour or pencil, he has used oil, and the pictures are uniformly of small size. The colour, representing Oxford in the brilliant sunlight of last August and September, is gay and sometimes splendid … It is a pity that a few of the pictures should have been put into common and rather gaudy frames of a 'fancy' German pattern."

Although principally a watercolour artist, Fulleylove often painted in oil and contributed oil paintings to the Royal Academy. But he himself regarded his black and white sketches more highly than his colour work.

Fulleylove contributed to various magazines, including the *Illustrated London News* and the *Magazine of Art*. He also illustrated a range of books, including H.W. Nevinson's *Pictures of Classic Greek Landscape and Architecture*

(1897), as well as *The Holy Land* (1902), *Oxford* (1903) and *Greece* (1906) in A&C Black's *Twenty Shilling Series* of colour plate books. He also provided the illustrations for four books in the same publisher's *7s 6d Series*: *Edinburgh* (1904), *Westminster Abbey* (1904), *Middlesex* (1907) and *The Tower of London* (1908). His paintings for *The Holy Land* were much reproduced as postcards by A&C Black as well as by Raphael Tuck. He also illustrated Richard Davey's *The Pageant of London* for Methuen.

John Fulleylove's output in the years 1902–8 was prolific – seven books for A&C Black alone – but his health faded quickly and he died on 22 May 1908. He was buried in Highgate Cemetery.

His entry in the *Dictionary of National Biography*, the source for some of the information above, refers to him as "an admirable architectural draughtsman … His water-colour was always laid over a solid and carefully completed pencil sketch. In colour his earlier works are silvery, sometimes a little weak, but always harmonious." His obituary in the *Art Journal* referred to him as "among the most distinguished architectural draughtsman of our time". It is this area of his art that seems to have gained most praise from contemporary critics and which resulted in *Greece* and *Oxford* being regarded as the most successful of his book illustrations.

Works by John Fulleylove can be found in collections and galleries in Cardiff, Leicester, Magdalen College, Oxford, and the Victoria & Albert Museum. One of the paintings from *The Holy Land* fetched £3,500 at auction in 2003, and a watercolour of Hampton Court Palace £1,600 in 2004.

The Parthenon from the North End of the Eastern Portico of the Propylaea, from *Greece*, 1906 (top); Westminster Abbey: The North Transept, from *Westminster Abbey*, 1914.

PLATE 1

THE CLARENDON BUILDING, BROAD STREET

Imposing buildings and serious-looking academics present a partial view of life in Oxford during the Edwardian era.

Close to the heart of the University, the Clarendon Building dominates this scene, its fine classical features conveying the message that Oxford is no ordinary city.

The eighteenth-century Clarendon Building – designed by Nicholas Hawksmoor – was originally constructed to house the Oxford University Press, which had outgrown its space in the nearby Sheldonian Theatre. However, by 1830 the Press again required more space and moved to its current premises in Walton Street. It is now one of the largest publishers in the UK and the largest university press in the world. The Clarendon Building now houses the University Library Service, the Press Delegates' Room, and the Vice-Chancellor's Robing Room.

At the street corner and on the steps of the Clarendon Building, Fellows in academic gowns are deep in conversation. It might be about something as trivial as when the next collection will be made from the nearby post box, but this is Oxford and one suspects that they are discussing something far less mundane.

Although Fulleylove's main interest seems to have been the life and architecture of the University, he does occasionally include a glimpse of "town" life such as the woman and child walking past a row of shops on the opposite side of the street. During the early twentieth century these included a hairdresser, a stationer and newsagent, a picture frame-maker and, as today, the main branch of Blackwell's bookshop.

PLATE 2

OXFORD, FROM THE SHELDONIAN THEATRE

This skyline view shows the pinnacles of the Bodleian Library, the dome of the Radcliffe Library, the spire of the University Church of St Mary, and Merton College tower

Over the centuries several locations in Oxford have provided views that have inspired poets. One of these, William Wordsworth, wrote:

> Yet, O ye spires of Oxford! Domes and towers!
> Gardens and groves! Your presence overpowers
> The soberness of reason ...

In Edwardian times this spectacular view from the octagonal cupola of the Sheldonian Theatre, situated at the heart of the University, was considered the best. The cupola was a mid-nineteenth-century addition to Christopher Wren's first architectural scheme, completed in 1669.

The Sheldonian's ornately painted ceiling is also not to be missed, and is one of the architectural jewels of Oxford. In the early twentieth century the Sheldonian curators, recognising the ceiling's artistic and architectural merit, arranged for its panels to be removed for repair. When they were replaced in 1901, a workman named Frank Morrill secretly left a package hidden behind one of the ceiling panels. Discovered over a hundred years later, this Edwardian time capsule included a pair of workman's trousers, some tools, and a letter asking for the trousers to be handed over to a local museum!

Clarendon Press and Sheldonian Theatre, Oxford

Oxford, Sheldonian Theatre

SPIRES OF OXFORD

PLATE 3

BISHOP HEBER'S TREE

Trees enhance many Oxford vistas, and this magnificent chestnut tree in Exeter College Fellows' Garden
was a feature of the north-west corner of Radcliffe Square for more than two hundred years.

Chestnut trees still grow in the Exeter College Garden, but none match the spread of this one planted in 1771. It was named after Reginald Heber, later Bishop of Calcutta, a student at nearby Brasenose College, whose rooms overlooked the garden and who became particularly fond of this tree.

It was said that if the tree's branches grew to touch Brasenose College wall, Exeter would defeat Brasenose at rowing that year. Did any superstitious Brasenose students breathe a sigh of relief when the ancient chestnut finally had to be cut down in 2005, more than a hundred years after this painting was completed?

A raised terrace inside the ancient walls of the garden provides a grandstand view of Radcliffe Square and the Italianate Radcliffe Camera, which is now part of the Bodleian Library.

Fans of fantasy writing may be interested to know that both J.R.R. Tolkien, author of *The Lord of the Rings*, and Philip Pullman were undergraduates at Exeter, which inspired Pullman's Jordan College in the trilogy *His Dark Materials*.

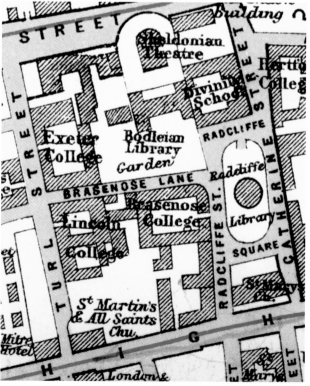

PLATE 4

ST EDMUND'S HALL

Popularly known as "Teddy Hall", St Edmund Hall (misspelled above in Edward Thomas's 1903 text)
is the oldest academic house in the University of Oxford.

This graveyard, linked to the college quadrangle by passageways through the building shown on the right, creates a quiet haven around the deconsecrated church of St Peter's in the East, which has become the college library.

St Edmund Hall has a history dating to the thirteenth century, and is the sole survivor of the medieval academic halls that preceded the foundation of the University. This is reflected in its name, retained even when St Edmund Hall was finally awarded college status in 1957 and became the only University college not to bear the name of "College".

The first decade of the twentieth century was a worrying one for the Fellows of St Edmund Hall. It seemed likely that Queen's College might absorb its much smaller neighbour when the Principal, Edward Moore, resigned. He

therefore postponed his departure for another ten years until 1912, by which time, after much campaigning, the University agreed to "the continuance of the Hall as a place of education, religion and learning separate from The Queen's College".

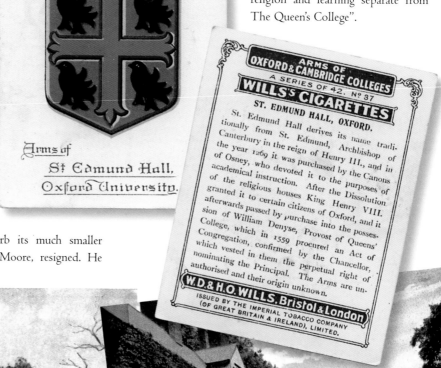

Wills's Cigarettes.

Arms of
St Edmund Hall,
Oxford University.

ARMS OF
OXFORD & CAMBRIDGE COLLEGES
A SERIES OF 42. No 37
WILLS'S CIGARETTES
ST. EDMUND HALL, OXFORD.
St. Edmund Hall derives its name traditionally from St. Edmund, Archbishop of Canterbury in the reign of Henry III., and in the year 1269 it was purchased by the Canons of Osney, who devoted it to the purposes of academical instruction. After the Dissolution of the religious houses King Henry VIII. granted it to certain citizens of Oxford, and it afterwards passed by purchase into the possession of William Denyse, Provost of Queens' College, which in 1559 procured an Act of Congregation, confirmed by the Chancellor, which vested in them the perpetual right of nominating the Principal. The Arms are unauthorised and their origin unknown.
W.D. & H.O. WILLS, Bristol & London
ISSUED BY THE IMPERIAL TOBACCO COMPANY
(OF GREAT BRITAIN & IRELAND), LIMITED.

PLATE 5

THE UNIVERSITY CHURCH OF ST MARY

The church of St Mary the Virgin has been at the centre
of University life since medieval times.

This partial view of St Mary's, showing the top of the tower, its pinnacles and spire, was painted from just outside the Canterbury Gate of Christ Church. The thirteenth-century tower is one of the best places to visit for spectacular views of Oxford, but climbing the more than 120 steps to the top must have presented a challenge for long-skirted Edwardian ladies. Stretching high above is the tallest of Oxford's "dreaming spires", which was built shortly after the tower and carefully restored in 1895.

Here a robed Fellow entering Oriel Square passes by a little lad in a knickerbocker suit and "butcher's boy" cap more reminiscent of Victorian times. Perhaps some errand has brought him from the busy High Street to the more exclusive college-lined streets.

St Mary's functions as both a parish and official University church, a relationship dating to medieval times, when this centrally located church was the focus of much academic life. Before the building of suitable University property, St Mary's was its seat of government, a chamber for debate, and a place for awarding degrees. In addition, an adjoining property housed the first University library and the University money chest.

PLATE 6

IFFLEY CHURCH FROM THE SOUTH-EAST

Now a leafy suburb of Oxford, at the beginning of the twentieth century
Iffley was a village lying within sight of the city spires.

The little parish church of St Mary the Virgin, standing on high ground overlooking the River Thames, boasts architecture to rival some of the grander University buildings a couple of miles away. One of the finest examples of romanesque architecture in Britain, the church's main beauty lies in its striking late-Norman carvings, inside and out, particularly around the south and west doors.

Visitors to the church will find the churchyard with its preaching cross and ancient yew tree little changed today. However, there is a more recent and notable addition to the building – a beautiful stained-glass window entitled "Nativity". Designed by John Piper, this was given to the church in 1995.

John Fulleylove must surely have visited the picturesque water mill that stood beside the river below the church, yet unlike many other artists he does not appear to have painted this ancient building. Dating to the mid-eleventh century, the mill was used for grinding local farmers' crops until it was burned out in a dramatic fire on 20 May 1908.

PLATE 7

TOM TOWER, CHRIST CHURCH COLLEGE

This tower and gateway create an impressive entrance to Oxford's largest college.

This magnificent gateway is a landmark on the Oxford skyline and the image that springs to mind for many when they hear the name "Oxford". It is regarded as one of the finest structures in the city, yet it was once far more modest. Built in the time of the founder, Cardinal Wolsey, in the sixteenth century, the original gateway was skilfully added to by Christopher Wren more than a hundred years later.

Tom Tower is named after one of the bells brought to the College from Osney Abbey in 1546. It was recast in 1680 and bears a Latin inscription that refers to "Great Tom, the door-closer of Oxford". In the 1900s, as in previous centuries, the "door-closer" still rang out at nine each night to mark the University curfew; undergraduates would be seen hurrying back to their colleges and the custodians would then close the college gates.

Anyone observing this, hearing the great bell sound 101 times (recalling the original number of college scholars) and glancing at his pocket watch, would have found that the time was actually five past nine. This was because Oxford lies five minutes west of Greenwich, and Great Tom retained the tradition of "Oxford time" being five minutes behind "Greenwich time".

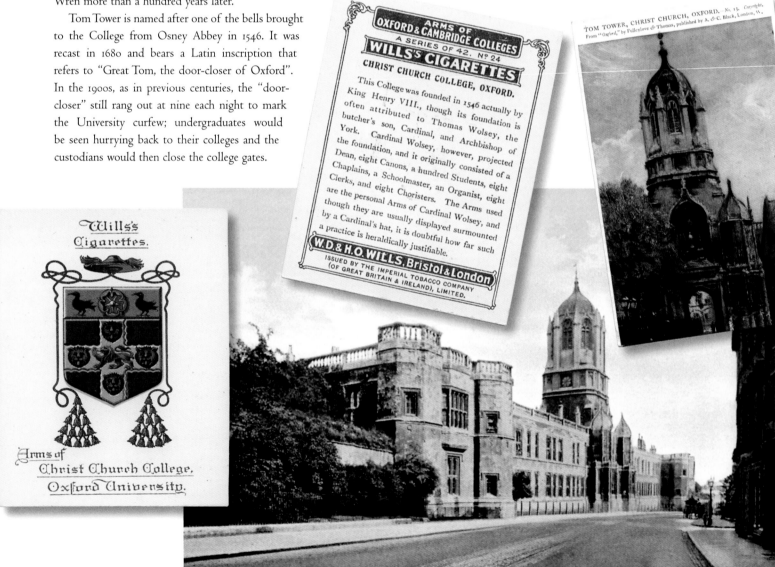

ARMS OF
OXFORD & CAMBRIDGE COLLEGES
A SERIES OF 42. No 24
WILL'S'S CIGARETTES
CHRIST CHURCH COLLEGE, OXFORD.
This College was founded in 1546 actually by King Henry VIII, though its foundation is often attributed to Thomas Wolsey, the butcher's son, Cardinal, and Archbishop of York. Cardinal Wolsey, however, projected the foundation, and it originally consisted of a Dean, eight Canons, a hundred Students, eight Chaplains, a Schoolmaster, an Organist, eight Clerks, and eight Choristers. The Arms used are the personal Arms of Cardinal Wolsey, and though they are usually displayed surmounted by a Cardinal's hat, it is doubtful how far such a practice is heraldically justifiable.
W.D. & H.O. WILLS, Bristol & London
ISSUED BY THE IMPERIAL TOBACCO COMPANY (OF GREAT BRITAIN & IRELAND), LIMITED.

TOM TOWER, CHRIST CHURCH, OXFORD. No. 11. Copyright.
From "Oxford," by Fulleylove & Thomas, published by A. & C. Black, London, W.

Wills's Cigarettes.

Arms of Christ Church College, Oxford University.

PLATE 8

ST GILES'S, LOOKING TOWARDS ST MARY MAGDALEN (SOUTH)

This broad, tree-lined highway runs from the medieval church of St Giles
in the north to the Martyrs' Memorial in the south.

The hansom cab waiting outside a recently constructed cab shelter is perhaps an early indication of how busy this spacious thoroughfare would become in later years. The shelter was also used as a temporary police station during the annual St Giles' Fair, an event which continues to attract crowds of people each September.

Visitors to Oxford in the early twentieth century would have found many attractions at the southern end of St Giles. These included the recently opened "new" Ashmolean Museum, which merged with the University's art gallery in 1908, and the Martyrs' Memorial, erected in 1841 to commemorate the deaths of the three sixteenth-century protestant leaders Cranmer, Latimer and Ridley. An ideal venue for refreshment, the elegant Randolph Hotel was conveniently placed just across the road.

In this painting, the entrance of St John's College, whose extensive properties line much of St Giles, can be glimpsed behind the trees on the left. On the opposite side of the road is The Eagle and Child, a pub favoured in later years by J.R.R. Tolkien, C.S. Lewis, Charles Williams and the other "Inklings".

RANDOLPH HOTEL, OXFORD.
In the Centre of the City, opposite the Martyrs' Memorial.
The only modern-built Hotel in Oxford, close to the Colleges and Public Buildings. A few minutes' walk from the Railway Stations, River, Theatre, &c.
Handsome Suites of Rooms. Ladies' Coffee Room. Ball Room. Billiard Rooms.
Smoking Rooms. General Drawing Room, and every convenience.
A Night Porter in attendance. Charges Moderate. American Elevator. Telephone, 32.
Address: Miss M. J. CREWE.

PLATE 9

CHRIST CHURCH –
INTERIOR OF LATIN CHAPEL

The chapel is dedicated to St Catherine of Alexandria, but became more commonly known
as the Latin Chapel as Latin prayers were once said here daily.

This fourteenth-century chapel to the north of the chancel contains a number of stained-glass windows depicting saints, but it is most closely associated with St Frideswide, who was buried at this site and is now the patron saint of both Oxford and the University. Scenes from her life are depicted in the colourful east window – shown here – which evokes something of the spirit of medieval stained glass but is actually much more modern, having been designed by Edward Burne-Jones and executed by William Morris in 1858.

At the centre of the painting, behind a pillar, are the remains of the richly carved stone shrine of St Frideswide, dating from the thirteenth century but destroyed some three centuries later. In Edwardian times this was a great attraction to visitors, as it had been possible to reconstruct parts of the shrine following their exciting discovery in the late nineteenth century,

A more recent reconstruction, with the addition of newly discovered pieces, can today be seen in the Latin Chapel. The carving on stone fragments is remarkable for its detailed and naturalistic representation of flowers and foliage, which include maple, columbine, celandine, hawthorn, bryony, sycamore, oak, vine, and ivy leaves.

PLATE 10

ST PETER'S-IN-THE-EAST

Records of a church standing on this site can be found
in the early eleventh-century Domesday Book.

"Like so much that is worth seeing, St Peter's in the East is hidden away … down a little lane which is what Oxford used to be like before the petrol age … The church itself is like a village church set down unexpectedly in a town." Writing in a guide to the church some fifty years after Fulleylove was painting, Sir John Betjeman thus captured the essence of this peaceful scene. It is little changed even today, although the building is now used as the library of St Edmund ("Teddy") Hall.

A former parishioner buried in this churchyard is James Sadler (1751–1828), the "first English aeronaut", whose family were pastry cooks in the nearby High Street. Ascending from Oxford in a hot air balloon in 1784, he reached a height of 3,600 feet and came down some six miles from the city near Woodeaton. It was not until a century after his death that a fitting memorial tablet was erected on this site.

PLATE 11

UNIVERSITY COLLEGE – PRIVATE GARDEN OF THE MASTER

The Master's lodging in Logic Lane overlooked these peaceful gardens and the college chapel.

Only a bay window (on the right) of the Master's charming Cotswold manor house "lodging", one of the benefits of his position as Head of College, can be seen in this painting. The east end of University College chapel, which houses seven wonderful painted windows by Abraham van Ling, dating from the seventeenth century, can be seen on the left.

As with all Oxford colleges, University College alumni include both the famous and the infamous. Clement Attlee (1883–1967), the post-war Labour Prime Minister who oversaw the introduction of the National Health Service and the granting of independence to India, came up as an undergraduate in 1901.

Some eight years later the College admitted an illustrious undergraduate from Russia, Prince Felix Youssoupoff, who is reputed to have been the richest student ever to have attended Oxford University. He was infamous at Oxford for the lavishness of his lifestyle, but in 1916 achieved even greater notoriety as the murderer of Rasputin.

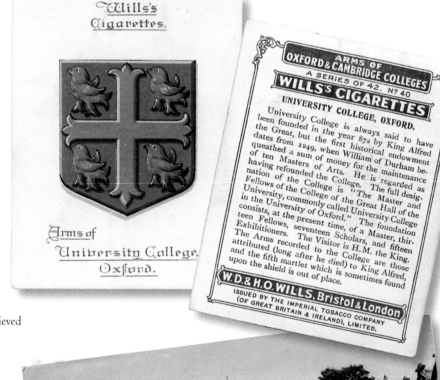

Wills's Cigarettes.

Arms of University College, Oxford.

ARMS OF OXFORD & CAMBRIDGE COLLEGES
A SERIES OF 42. Nº 40
WILL'S CIGARETTES

UNIVERSITY COLLEGE, OXFORD.

University College is always said to have been founded in the year 872 by King Alfred the Great, but the first historical endowment dates from 1249, when William of Durham bequeathed a sum of money for the maintenance of ten Masters of Arts. He is regarded as having refounded the College. The full designation of the College is "The Master and Fellows of the College of the Great Hall of the University, commonly called University College in the University of Oxford." The foundation consists, at the present time, of a Master, thirteen Fellows, seventeen Scholars, and fifteen Exhibitioners. The Visitor is H.M. the King. The Arms recorded to the College are those attributed (long after he died) to King Alfred, and the fifth martlet which is sometimes found upon the shield is out of place.

W.D.& H.O.WILLS, Bristol & London
ISSUED BY THE IMPERIAL TOBACCO COMPANY (OF GREAT BRITAIN & IRELAND), LIMITED.

University College

Stengel & Co. Dresden-Berlin 19359

PLATE 12

MERTON COLLEGE AND ST ALBAN'S HALL

Founded in 1264, Merton College is the oldest of the Oxford colleges.

Oxford colleges are famous for their quadrangles and Merton College, despite its relatively small site between the city walls and Merton Street, now boasts no fewer than four such courtyards. The Mob Quad is probably the best known, although the entrance or Front Quad shown here is reckoned to pre-date the more obscurely named courtyard.

The rooftops of St Alban's Hall can be seen above the building in the north-east corner, to the left. This "academic hall" had been absorbed into Merton in the 1880s, and was demolished shortly after Fulleylove completed this painting to make way for the construction of what is now St Alban's Quad.

In 1907 Basil Henry Blackwell (1889–1984), son of the founder of the now internationally famous Blackwell's Bookshop in Broad Street, was awarded a scholarship to Merton. He went on to found his own publishing group and was head of the family firm for more than sixty years.

Wills's Cigarettes.

Arms of
Merton College.
Oxford University.

MERTON COLLEGE
OXFORD
H.J.White·M·A·

ARMS OF OXFORD & CAMBRIDGE COLLEGES

A SERIES OF 42. No 32

WILLS'S CIGARETTES

MERTON COLLEGE, OXFORD.

Merton College was originally founded at Malden, in Surrey, in 1264, and called "The House of Scholars of Merton." It was founded by Walter de Merton, Lord Chancellor of England, and afterwards Bishop of Rochester, and in 1274 the whole community of the College was permanently settled in Oxford. The Scholarships, known at this College as Post-masterships, are twenty in number, and are each worth about £80 per annum. Most of these are awarded as the result of examinations. The Arms illustrated, which were recorded to the College at the Heralds' Visitation in 1574, are the personal Arms of the founder, but they are often used in conjunction with the Arms of the See of Rochester.

W.D. & H.O. WILLS, Bristol & London
ISSUED BY THE IMPERIAL TOBACCO COMPANY (OF GREAT BRITAIN & IRELAND), LIMITED.

PLATE 13

ORIEL COLLEGE

Oriel's ornate Front Quad dates to the seventeenth century and was the result of rebuilding,
a regular occurrence as the college continued its expansion over the centuries.

The start of the Edwardian era proved significant for Oriel College. In 1902 the College united with the adjoining St Mary Hall – the fourth of the original medieval halls to be incorporated within Oriel. This virtually doubled student numbers, and it became obvious that redevelopment work was necessary.

However, in the same year the College received a timely bequest of £100,000 from the wealthy colonialist Cecil Rhodes, a former undergraduate at Oriel. This

was perhaps received with more enthusiasm than Rhodes himself had been – at the time of his admission the College President is reputed to have grumbled, "all the colleges send me their failures". By 1909 this legacy had enabled Oriel to commence redevelopment of part of St Mary Hall, with the new Rhodes Building creating much needed additional residential accommodation for their students.

This significant bequest was not Rhodes' only legacy. He also left a larger bequest – a considerable fortune – to establish a scholarship programme, thus founding the world's first international fellowship, the Rhodes Scholarship, which continues to bring outstanding students from around the world to Oxford to this day.

Wills's
Cigarettes.

Arms of
Oriel College.
Oxford University.

ARMS OF
OXFORD & CAMBRIDGE COLLEGES
A SERIES OF 42. No 34
WILL'S CIGARETTES

ORIEL COLLEGE, OXFORD.

Oriel College is sometimes said to have been founded by Adam le Brome, Clerk in the Chancery, and Confessor to King Edward II., but it was really founded by that King himself in 1326, on the suggestion of his Confessor, for a Provost and ten Fellows. During the period between 1445 and 1529 large additional endowments were given to the College by its successive Provosts—John Frank, Master of the Rolls; John Carpenter, Bishop of Worcester; Walter Lyhert, Bishop of Norwich; and John Hals, Bishop of Coventry and Lichfield. The Arms of the College are a differenced version of the Arms of King Edward II., and were recorded in 1574 at the Heralds' Visitation of the County of Oxford.

W.D.& H.O. WILLS, Bristol & London
ISSUED BY THE IMPERIAL TOBACCO COMPANY
(OF GREAT BRITAIN & IRELAND), LIMITED.

PLATE 14

GROVE STREET

Now called Magpie Lane, this ancient thoroughfare runs from
the High Street, opposite St Mary's Church, south to Merton Street.

Central Oxford has long been full of quaint lanes and narrow streets. One of these is Grove Street, whose name is thought to date back to the thirteenth century, when the disreputable thoroughfare was known as Grope Lane, a name used widely in the Middle Ages for a place where prostitutes conducted their business. By Fulleylove's time, however, the street had taken on a far more respectable character.

At the High Street end, the street is little more than a pedestrianised alleyway. It broadens to the south, finally opening out onto Merton Street, the only road in Oxford still paved with original cobblestones. The lane continues to the south of Merton Street, where it was known as Grove Walk (now Merton Grove), and leads to one of the gates of Christ Church Meadow.

During the seventeenth and eighteenth centuries the thoroughfare was named Magpie Lane after a local alehouse, an identity that was readopted in the late 1920s and continues to this day.

Merton Tower, Oxford.

PLATE 15

NEW COLLEGE

New College is actually one of the oldest colleges in the University, but to avoid confusion
with what is now Oriel College it changed its original name in about 1400.

Wills's
Cigarettes.

MANNERS MAKYTH MAN.

Arms of
New College.
Oxford University.

ARMS OF
OXFORD & CAMBRIDGE COLLEGES
A SERIES OF 42. No 33
WILLS'S CIGARETTES
NEW COLLEGE, OXFORD.

New College, Oxford, was founded in 1379
by William of Wykeham, Bishop of Winchester,
and Lord Chancellor of England, for a Warden,
seventy Fellows and Scholars, ten Chaplains,
three Clerks, and sixteen Choristers, and its
proper description is "The Warden and Scholars
of St. Mary College of Winchester in Oxford,
commonly called New College in Oxford."
William of Wykeham also founded Winchester
School, and each year six Winchester Scholarships are available at New College for those
who have been educated at Winchester. The
Arms recorded for New College are the Wykeham Arms, with their famous motto "Manners
makyth man," which School and College use in
common.

W.D.& H.O.WILLS, Bristol & London
ISSUED BY THE IMPERIAL TOBACCO COMPANY
(OF GREAT BRITAIN & IRELAND), LIMITED.

NEW COLLEGE
OXFORD
A.O.Prickard

The
College

MONOGR

In parts of New College it is possible to imagine oneself on the
site of an ancient castle. In fact the large mound in the Garden
Quad is a relic of what was once a formal garden, and the massive
stone walls are part of Oxford's old city wall. It was
in a building on the other side of these
walls that William Morris set up his garage
in 1910. Only two years later he produced
the first "Morris-Oxford light car" – and
the rest is history.

Many heads of Oxford colleges are quickly
forgotten, but the New College Warden
in the Edwardian era has since become a
household name. William Spooner was a gifted
and popular Warden but prone to accidentally
transposing the initial sounds of words, thus
creating a "spoonerism". There are many
apocryphal spoonerisms, but among those believed
to be authentic are – when announcing
a hymn in chapel – "Kinquering Congs
their titles take"; and – when chastising
an undergraduate – "You have deliberately
tasted two worms and you can leave
Oxford by the town drain". It was a harsh
punishment; did the student manage to
keep a straight face?

PLATE 16

INTERIOR OF THE BODLEIAN LIBRARY

Duke Humfrey's Library is named after the benefactor who presented
the University with three hundred books in the late fifteenth century.

The library painted by Fulleylove is now a reading room of the Bodleian Library, a copyright deposit library and one of the greatest libraries in the world. The librarian at the turn of the twentieth century was Edward Williams Byron Nicholson, a characterful figure with a constantly tumbling monacle who was described as "a tornado, the billowing sleeves of his gown scattering the papers of library readers as he dashed down Duke Humphrey (sic)".

Nicholson's "sole aim and passion was to extend the usefulness of the great library". He worked towards this goal with dedication, often creating controversy, particularly in his latter years.

With usefulness uppermost in his mind, in 1907 he engaged staff to begin creating a uniform library catalogue, and by 1909 was optimistically forecasting that the first part of letter A would be completed within five years. Unsurprisingly the task proved far greater than anticipated, and a comprehensive catalogue was not available until decades later.

By the early twentieth century the Bodleian was doubling its size within a generation, and the library's records show that in 1911 alone it received almost 74,000 items. Nicholson therefore proposed the construction of an underground storage room with space-saving movable "book stacks", and work to build these under part of Radcliffe Square was begun in 1909. Unfortunately he did not live to see completion of this project in 1912.

PLATE 17

INTERIOR OF THE LIBRARY, ALL SOULS' COLLEGE

A statue of Sir Christopher Codrington stands in the centre of the impressive library that he founded.

The Codrington Library was funded by a generous bequest on the death of Sir Christopher Codrington, Governor-General of the Leeward Islands, in 1710. Unlike many libraries, this is spacious and airy, and the tall windows in the south wall and at either end provide plenty of light – enhanced by the introduction of artificial lighting in 1909 – for those studying there. Unusually for the time, the library was at ground level rather than on the first floor, with a brick vault to guard against the damp.

Codrington not only paid for the construction of the library but also added many books, on a wide range of subjects, to the college's already significant collection of books and manuscripts.

The library gained recognition for its growing collection of law and history texts, but it was not until 1903 that it again had the opportunity for significant expansion. In this year a donation of £2,000 from an anonymous Edwardian benefactor funded the purchase of several thousand much-needed history books in French, Italian and German.

At a time when the wages of some non-academic staff must have been calculated in only shillings a week, this expenditure might have seemed enormously extravagant. Others would argue that an Oxford education has had inestimable value for many thousands of individuals around the world since then, and will continue to do so for many years to come.

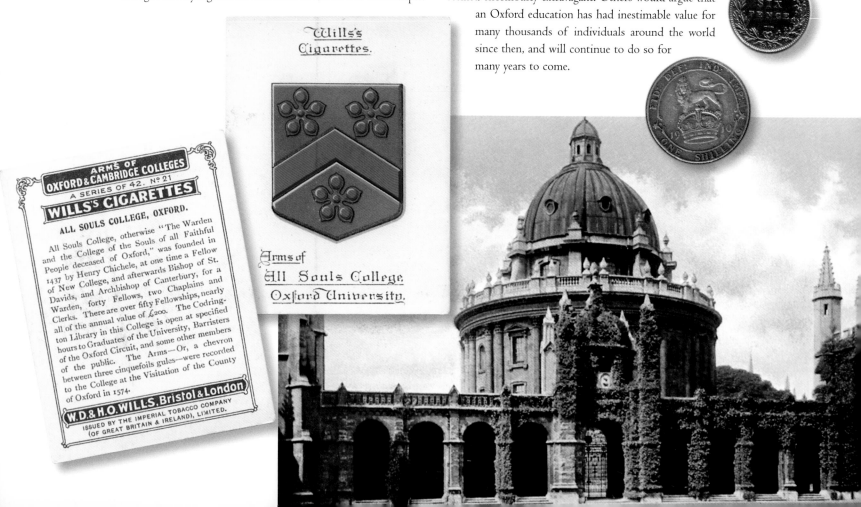

PLATE 18

THE CLOISTERS, MAGDALEN COLLEGE

Attached to the President's Lodgings, the Hall and the Chapel,
the Cloisters have long been at the heart of Magdalen College.

Magdalen (pronounced "Maudlin") College is considered by many to be the most beautiful college in Oxford, and one of its most admired features is the fifteenth-century cloistered quad. Having suffered sometimes unsympathetic alterations over the previous centuries, much of the cloister's original medieval character was restored in the early nineteenth century.

Quiet is encouraged in the cloisters and, being there, one could almost imagine being inside a peaceful medieval monastery. The strange allegorical figures and gargoyles on the cloister buttresses seem rather at odds with the rest of the architecture, and some are said to have been an inspiration to author C.S. Lewis for the stone statues in the land of Narnia – Lewis was a Fellow of English Language and Literature at Magdalen from 1925 to 1954.

Do the figures in academic dress seen standing on the grassy quad, something that would be frowned upon in modern times, include Herbert Warren, Magdalen's President in the Edwardian era? He is credited with turning around the College's academic profile and making it one of the most prestigious Oxford colleges of the time. His work did not go unnoticed, and the admission of the Prince of Wales, later Edward VIII, to the college in 1912, was a clear mark of his success.

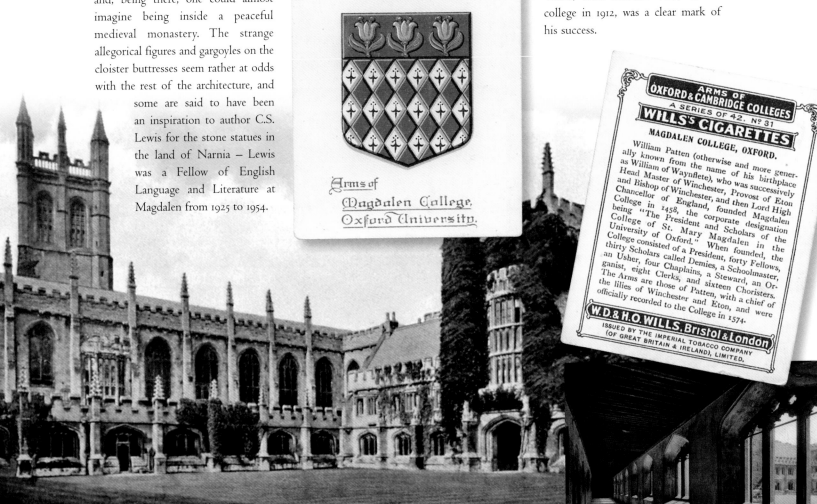

Wills's
Cigarettes.

Arms of
Magdalen College,
Oxford University.

ARMS OF
OXFORD & CAMBRIDGE COLLEGES
A SERIES OF 42. No 31
WILLS'S CIGARETTES
MAGDALEN COLLEGE, OXFORD.

William Patten (otherwise and more generally known from the name of his birthplace as William of Waynflete), who was successively Head Master of Winchester, Provost of Eton and Bishop of Winchester, and then Lord High Chancellor of England, founded Magdalen College in 1458, the corporate designation being "The President and Scholars of the College of St. Mary Magdalen in the University of Oxford." When founded, the College consisted of a President, forty Fellows, thirty Scholars called Demies, a Schoolmaster, an Usher, four Chaplains, a Steward, an Organist, eight Clerks, and sixteen Choristers. The Arms are those of Patten, with a chief of the lilies of Winchester and Eton, and were officially recorded to the College in 1574.

W.D.& H.O. WILLS, Bristol & London
ISSUED BY THE IMPERIAL TOBACCO COMPANY
(OF GREAT BRITAIN & IRELAND), LIMITED.

PLATE 19

ST JOHN'S COLLEGE

From the confines of the college's ornate, arcaded Canterbury Quad
a small gate opens out onto this broad expanse of lawn.

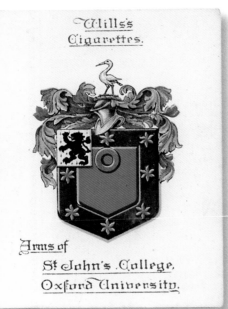

The garden of St John's is one of the most beautiful and extensive in Oxford. Its layout still reflects the influence of the landscaping movement which dominated English garden design in the late eighteenth century, though by Edwardian times many more shrubs and trees had been added. The main feature has always been the lawn, which extends from the buildings along St Giles to Parks Road in the east. In addition to the usual team of gardeners and groundsmen, St John's also has the aptly named "Keeper of the Groves", who is one of the Fellows.

The University has always attracted students with an interest in politics and social reform. No fewer than twenty-five former Oxford graduates have become prime ministers, the first being the Earl of Wilmington (1673–1743) and the latest St John's alumnus Tony Blair (1997–2007).

Another notable former student at St John's was Fabian intellectual Sidney Ball, who was involved in the creation in 1903 of the Workers' Educational Association (WEA). This voluntary organisation, which continues its important work today, supported the educational needs of workers, and was much needed at a time when few working-class youngsters stayed at school beyond the age of fourteen.

Oxford. St John's College Gardens.

PLATE 20

MAGDALEN TOWER AND BOTANIC GARDEN

Oxford's open spaces range from the formality of the Botanic Garden and
University Parks to the bucolic informality of the riverside meadows.

Even in the 1900s, people sometimes found they
needed to get away from the hustle and bustle of
the city, and taking a relaxing stroll in one of
Oxford's many open spaces became a popular
pastime. It is likely that these two fashionably
dressed young ladies would not have been the
only people taking an early evening walk in
the meadows close to the Botanic Garden.

Among the other popular walking
destinations were the larger University Parks and
the common ground of Port Meadow. There were
footpaths marking popular routes around Christ Church
Meadow, along Dead Man's Walk, and the river walks beside the
Cherwell and Thames.

The tower of Magdalen College serves as a
reminder of the college's long association
with the Botanic Garden. Magdalen was the
first college to teach science, and it was the
presence of many early physicians at the
college that led to the establishment, in 1621,
of what was then called the Physic Garden
on Magdalen land.

THE BOTANIC GARDENS, OXFORD.

L.WHASLEHURST.

PLATE 21

MAGDALEN TOWER AND BRIDGE

The soaring tower of Magdalen College overlooks the main road
taken by travellers approaching Oxford from the east.

By the early twentieth century Magdalen Bridge had become a busy thoroughfare both for pedestrians and a varied range of transport. As well as goods vehicles and coaches carrying passengers from far afield, there were horse-drawn trams and buses that regularly carried passengers into the city from the expanding residential areas to the east of the city. There was also an increasing number of motor cars, including (from 1912) the locally built Morris-Oxford car from William Morris.

Here Fulleylove shows some buildings of the Botanic Garden, but it is the beautiful buildings to the right that are the focus of his painting. One cannot ignore Magdalen Tower — famous both for its beauty and for an annual event dating to the sixteenth century and continuing, in a slightly different form, to the present day. At 6 o'clock on May Day morning the Magdalen Choir ascends the 144-foot tower to sing a hymn to welcome the arrival of spring. Crowds of onlookers from both town and gown always gather below — in the High, the Botanic Garden and on Magdalen Bridge — to take part in the thanksgiving.

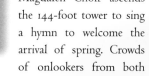

Wills's
Cigarettes.

Arms of
Magdalen College,
Oxford University.

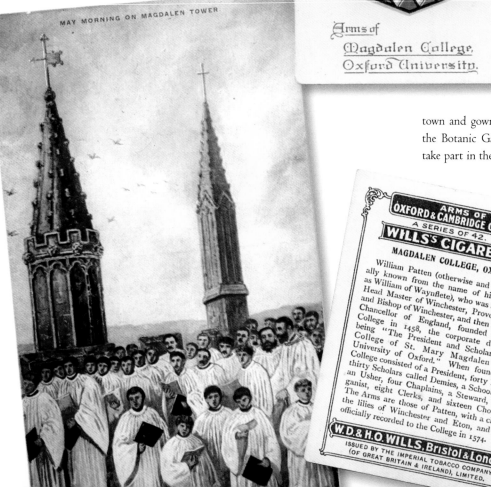

MAY MORNING ON MAGDALEN TOWER.

ARMS OF
OXFORD & CAMBRIDGE COLLEGES
A SERIES OF 42. No 31
WILLS'S CIGARETTES
MAGDALEN COLLEGE, OXFORD.
William Patten (otherwise and more gener-
ally known from the name of his birthplace
as William of Waynflete), who was successively
Head Master of Winchester, Provost of Eton
and Bishop of Winchester, and then Lord High
Chancellor of England, founded Magdalen
College in 1458, the corporate designation
being "The President and Scholars of the
College of St. Mary Magdalen in the
University of Oxford." When founded, the
College consisted of a President, forty Fellows,
thirty Scholars called Demies, a Schoolmaster,
an Usher, four Chaplains, a Steward, an Or-
ganist, eight Clerks, and sixteen Choristers.
The Arms are those of Patten, with a chief of
the lilies of Winchester and Eton, and were
officially recorded to the College in 1574.
W.D.& H.O. WILLS, Bristol & London
ISSUED BY THE IMPERIAL TOBACCO COMPANY
(OF GREAT BRITAIN & IRELAND), LIMITED.

Magdalen Bridge & Tower
Oxford Fullleylove

PLATE 22

ALL SOULS' COLLEGE
AND THE HIGH STREET

The architecture of Oxford's High Street inspired Pevsner to describe it as "one of the world's greatest streets".

At the turn of the twentieth century anyone approaching Oxford along the High (as Oxford High Street is usually known) could hardly fail to have been impressed by its architecture, especially on a sunny day. In the days before pollution had left its mark on the city, the honey-coloured college and church buildings lining either side of the road would have had a warm, inviting glow about them.

The front of All Souls' College, on the right, dominates the foreground. Looking further west we see part of the south aisle of St Mary's Church and the white pinnacles of the nave, the elegant

tower and spire of All Saints, and the distant Carfax Tower, all that remained of the recently demolished St Martin's church.

A group of academics engrossed in conversation outside the entrance to All Souls seems oblivious to those making their way to and from the city centre. Clearly pedestrians were not confined to pavements before motor vehicles became commonplace, although anyone strolling along this highway needed to keep watch for the increasing amount of traffic. Horse-drawn trams from the rapidly developing areas of east Oxford, and horse-buses from the outlying soon-to-be suburbs of Headington and Iffley, ran regular services to bring passengers into the city.

Oxford, All Souls College from Radcliffe Camera (Founded A.D. 1437).

HIGH STREET, OXFORD

A.R.Q.

PLATE 23

INTERIOR OF THE SHELDONIAN THEATRE

The Sheldonian Theatre has been used for University ceremonies such as matriculation
and the awarding of degrees since the early eighteenth century.

"The ceremony was all most venerable and beautiful, and I was greatly moved by it." So said Samuel Langhorn Clemens, better known as American author Mark Twain, the day after receiving an honorary degree in 1907. Encaenia (a Greek term pronounced "enseenya", meaning "festival of dedication"), the event at which such degrees are conferred on selected famous people from all over the world, is the highlight of the academic year. It is a spectacular ceremony involving stately processions of dignitaries through the heart of the University, but it is in the Sheldonian Theatre that the degree ceremony itself takes place, following a traditional pattern of ritual and speeches, some in Latin, given from the high-level rostrum.

In Edwardian times the number of honorary degrees awarded each year was far greater than today with, for example, more than thirty being awarded in June 1907. Among the recipients of degrees on

CURE · LATIN ENTRY ROSTRUM · SHELDONIAN THEATRE · 1904.

the same morning as Clemens were Prime Minister Campbell-Bannerman, Rudyard Kipling, Auguste Rodin, and General William Booth of the Salvation Army.

In addition to official University uses of the Sheldonian, the building has long been available to the public for concerts and meetings. Any decisions about whether or not to accept applications for such events are made by the Sheldonian's curators who, in the early twentieth century, were six in number and included the Vice-Chancellor of the University.

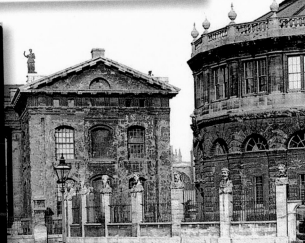

PLATE 24

CORPUS CHRISTI COLLEGE

The small college of Corpus Christi adjoins the largest, Christ Church,
yet it has an intimate beauty of its own.

Corpus Christi's gateway on Merton Street opens on to a small quadrangle with a central pillar surmounted by a statue of a pelican. From medieval times, this bird has been a Christian symbol of Christ's sacrifice, and was adopted as the symbol of Corpus Christi on its foundation in 1517.

On the pillar below the pelican is an ornate and complex dial with four main faces, one for each point of the compass.

Constructed in 1581, this dial made use of the latest scientific developments of the period, and can calculate time both by the sun and the moon. It is worth remembering that the dial is set to Oxford time, so it is always five minutes behind Greenwich mean time.

In 1904 a controversial new Corpus Christi President was appointed. Thomas Case was a traditionalist who "opposed changes in Church, State and university", and supported the exclusion of women from the University. His influence was long-lasting – Corpus Christi did not admit women students until 1979.

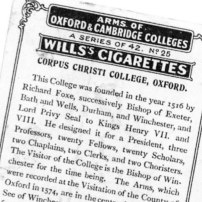

Wills's Cigarettes.

Arms of Corpus Christi College, Oxford University.

ARMS OF OXFORD & CAMBRIDGE COLLEGES
A SERIES OF 42. No. 25
WILL'S CIGARETTES
CORPUS CHRISTI COLLEGE, OXFORD.

This College was founded in the year 1516 by Richard Foxe, successively Bishop of Exeter, Bath and Wells, Durham, and Winchester, and Lord Privy Seal to Kings Henry VII. and VIII. He designed it for a President, three Professors, twenty Fellows, twenty Scholars, two Chaplains, two Clerks, and two Choristers. The Visitor of the College is the Bishop of Winchester for the time being. The Arms, which were recorded at the Visitation of the County of Oxford in 1574, are in the centre the Arms of the See of Winchester. The "pelican in her piety" forms the personal Coat of Arms of Richard Foxe, whilst the Arms on the sinister side are those of Hugh Oldham, Bishop of Exeter.

W.D.& H.O. WILLS. Bristol & London
ISSUED BY THE IMPERIAL TOBACCO COMPANY
(OF GREAT BRITAIN & IRELAND), LIMITED.

PLATE 25

CHRIST CHURCH – PECKWATER QUADRANGLE

Peckwater Quad was built in the early eighteenth century to provide
accommodation for the growing number of students at Christ Church.

Despite its name, Fulleylove's painting shows only a small portion
of this quad – which is built in classical style – seen through an
opening between some masters' houses on the left and the College
Library on the right. Unfortunately this view of the library does
not give a hint of the fine neo-classical frontage that can be
found just around the corner. Peckwater Quad is named after the
medieval Oxford family who had kept an inn on this site and later
given it to the nearby St Frideswide's priory.

Some of the finest rooms in Christ Church were on the first
floor of Peckwater Quad. Between the turn of the twentieth
century and the First World War many of them were allocated
to those undergraduates who were seen as giving the college an
air of grandeur. They included princes from Asia and the Far
East, Prussia and Russia, the sons of wealthy businessmen from
America and Greece, and the scions of English aristocrats.

It was in Peckwater Quad that, some 250 years earlier, William
Penn led a Puritan group objecting to the introduction of
surplices after the Restoration. What became known as "The
Surplice Riot" resulted in the future founder of Pennsylvania
being sent down from the University for non-conformity.

Oxford, Christ Church, Peckwater Quadrangle.

Peckwater Quadrangle, Christ Church, Oxford.

PLATE 26

THE RADCLIFFE LIBRARY, OR CAMERA BODLEIANA, FROM ALL SOULS' COLLEGE

The baroque Radcliffe Camera has been a distinctive feature of the Oxford skyline since 1749.

The great dome of the Radcliffe Library, which towers above the North Quad of All Souls College, is only one of the spectacular buildings to be seen from this location. The Quad itself contains a wealth of "Gothic" architecture designed by Nicholas Hawksmoor, including the exterior of the Codrington Library and the ornate pinnacled twin towers whose shadow falls across this scene.

All Souls is unique among Oxford colleges in having no undergraduate members – continuing a tradition from medieval times when the colleges were the sole preserve of graduates. Its Fellows, most of whom work in Oxford, are generally considered to be outstanding in their academic field. The college has many famous alumni, including Christopher Wren, whose influence is seen in much of the architecture of both University and city.

Life in the University has always had its lighter moments, not least at All Souls with its Mallard Day tradition. The warden leads a torchlit procession through the college to look for a mythical duck, supposedly discovered when the college was first being built, all the while singing the ancient "Mallard Song". This eccentric ritual takes place only once a century, and in 1905 college members had the rare opportunity to take part and revel in true Edwardian style.

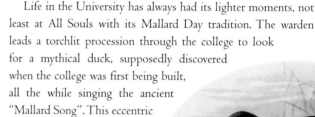

PLATE 27

ENTRANCE GATEWAY OF HERTFORD COLLEGE AND THE RADCLIFFE LIBRARY

Framed by a gateway, this glimpse of the Radcliffe Camera was shortly
to disappear as a result of college building developments.

Hertford College can lay claim to being one of the oldest Oxford colleges. Originally founded as Hart Hall in 1282, its name was changed to Hertford College in 1740, and it was finally established as a full college in 1874 after a long delay caused by funding problems.

In the early twentieth century much rebuilding took place at Hertford College, including the chapel, dedicated in 1908, and new college buildings on Catte Street. The spectacular "Bridge of Sighs", spanning New College Lane and linking two Hertford quads, was constructed shortly afterwards in 1913–14.

Hertford College has a tradition of being "progressive", and was among the first colleges to admit women undergraduates. However, much earlier, in 1907, it took what was then a more radical step in admitting their first African–American Rhodes Scholar. Alain Locke had been turned down by several colleges on grounds of race, and later went on to make a significant contribution to the philosophy, art, and culture of American society.

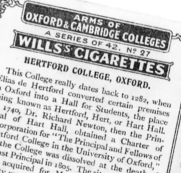

ARMS OF
OXFORD & CAMBRIDGE COLLEGES
A SERIES OF 42. № 27
WILLS's CIGARETTES
HERTFORD COLLEGE, OXFORD.

This College really dates back to 1282, when Elias de Hertford converted certain premises in Oxford into a Hall for Students, the place being known as Hertford, Hert, or Hart Hall. In 1740, Dr. Richard Newton, then the Principal of Hart Hall, obtained a Charter of Incorporation for "The Principal and Fellows of Hertford College in the University of Oxford," but the College was dissolved at the death of the last Principal in 1805. The site and buildings were acquired for Magdalen Hall, but that Society was dissolved in 1874 by Act of Parliament, and the Principal and Fellows were re-incorporated by certain other Fellows in 1874 by Act of Parliament, and the Principal and Fellows and Scholars of Hertford College in the University of Oxford." The Arms are not of official authority.

W.D.& H.O. WILLS Bristol & London
ISSUED BY THE IMPERIAL TOBACCO COMPANY (OF GREAT BRITAIN & IRELAND), LIMITED.

Wills's
Cigarettes.

Arms of
Hertford College,
Oxford University.

PLATE 28

INTERIOR OF THE CATHEDRAL OF CHRIST CHURCH

The twelfth-century Cathedral Church of Christ in Oxford is unique in being both the diocesan mother church and a college chapel.

The influence of the church on University life was still strong in Edwardian times, and undergraduates at Oxford were expected to attend their college chapel each day. Christ Church was one of the few colleges that still required its students to wear surplices for worship, a tradition that may have continued because their place of worship was no ordinary chapel, but also a cathedral.

As the cathedral followed "Oxford time", worshippers expecting evensong to begin at 6 p.m. had a further five minutes in which to meditate or to survey the surrounding architecture before the service began.

The beautiful rose window and the spectacular vaulting above the choir are just two of the cathedral's many notable features.

There has been a choir at the cathedral since 1526, when it was founded by Cardinal Wolsey. However, it was not until Dean Strong took up his post in 1901 that any head of college took an active interest in the cathedral choir. Strong encouraged ever higher standards, and is said to have nurtured the young William Walton, one of the most talented composers of his generation, whose first compositions were written while he was a pupil at the Cathedral School.

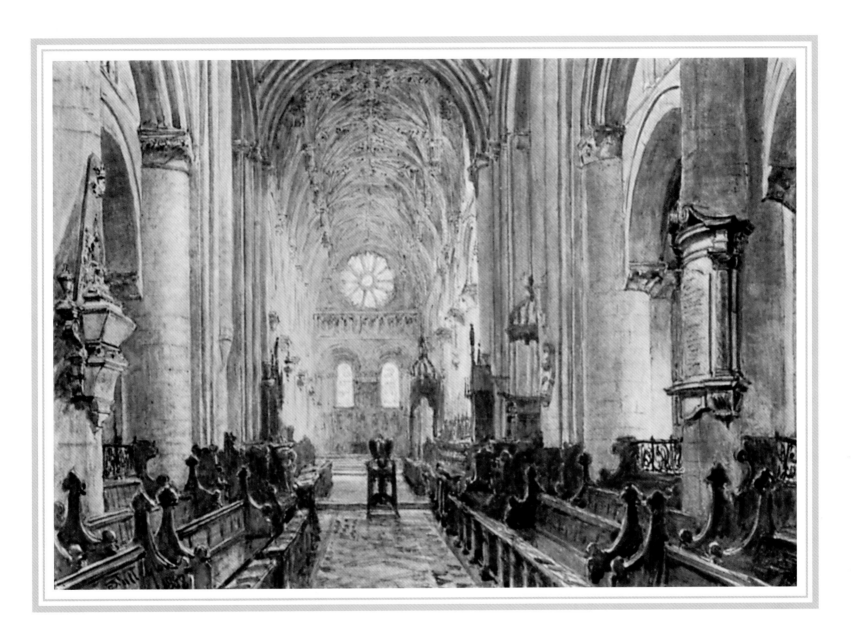

PLATE 29

MAGDALEN COLLEGE, FROM THE BOTANIC GARDEN

First established as a Physic Garden in the seventeenth century, Oxford's Botanic Garden had become a popular place for recreation by Edwardian times.

Here we see middle-class Edwardians at leisure on a summer's day. The exotic plants in one of the larger glasshouses have attracted several interested viewers, and a young couple relaxing on the shady grass are enjoying a freedom that might not have been acceptable in a public place in the previous century.

The earliest known conservatories date from the seventeenth century, and those in the Oxford Botanic Garden are believed to have been the first to be constructed in Britain. However, those shown here were constructed in 1893.

Close to Magdalen Bridge a young man is punting – a leisure activity that developed in the Thames valley in the 1860s when the demand for work-punts (used for such things as ferrying, fishing and dredging) declined. There were places on the Thames where punt-racing was a recognised sport, and a University punting championship took place in 1905, when races were held on the Thames alongside Port Meadow. As the event was never repeated it seems that Oxford students may have preferred a more sedate use of these craft.

PLATE 30

THE RADCLIFFE LIBRARY,
OR CAMERA BODLEIANA, FROM
BRASENOSE COLLEGE QUADRANGLE

The great dome of the Library rises above the gateway tower, dominating Radcliffe Square,
the Church of St Mary the Virgin, and the surrounding colleges.

The wonderful baroque Radcliffe Camera, believed to be the first round library in the country, is part of the Bodleian Library. It was originally intended to be a science library, but gradually its shelves were given over to books devoted to the arts. In the early twentieth century the Library was connected to the main Bodleian site by an underground tunnel, and a vault was created to store some 600,000 books beneath Radcliffe Square.

Just to the west, on Radcliffe Square, is the main entrance to Brasenose College, seen behind the group of figures in this painting, ideally placed for college members wanting to use any of the Bodleian Libraries. As well as producing academic successes, from the nineteenth century to the First World War Brasenose was notable for its students' prowess on the cricket and rugby pitches and on the river – it was Head of the River for many years and at one stage provided no fewer than eight members of the University cricket team.

Many Oxford colleges had their own traditions, and in 1909 Brasenose revived a Shrove Tuesday custom that dated back to when the College had a brewhouse (it had been demolished in 1889). Each year an undergraduate would write topical verses in praise of the Brasenose Ale, to be recited while the assembled company drank warmed beer with spice and apples. No doubt this was of more interest to the young Edwardian gentlemen than tossing pancakes would have been!

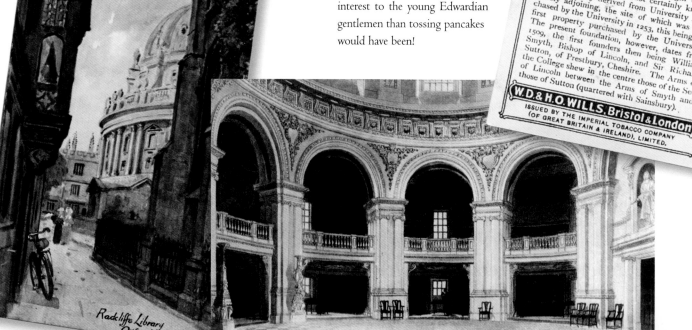

Radcliffe Library
Oxford

PLATE 31

BISHOP KING'S HOUSE

There are conflicting opinions about whether a bishop ever lived
in this building, which is also known as "The Old Palace".

This seventeenth-century mansion was built on the site of an earlier house said to have been occupied by Robert King, the last Abbot of Osney and first Bishop of Oxford. The frontage on St Aldate's is narrow, and the plot with its garden extends a long way back – telltale clues to the building's medieval origins.

By Fulleylove's time, the many-gabled building was in need of repair, and considerable refurbishment and redecoration was carried out in 1906. During work on the ornate plaster ceilings, builders discovered traces of charred beams and damaged plaster apparently dating back to the Civil War.

The white houses shown on the opposite side of St Aldate's were demolished in the 1920s to make way for a Garden of Remembrance in memory of the 225 Christ Church members who died in the First World War. An unplanned benefit was that this also created an excellent view and pathway through to Christ Church Meadow.

Nearby one can still find the "little dark shop" that provided inspiration for local author Lewis Carroll as the place in *Alice Through the Looking-Glass* where Alice meets a knitting sheep.

PLATE 32

THE CLARENDON BUILDING, LOOKING EAST

The stately Clarendon Building and the smaller Indian Institute create an attractive closure to the east end of Broad Street.

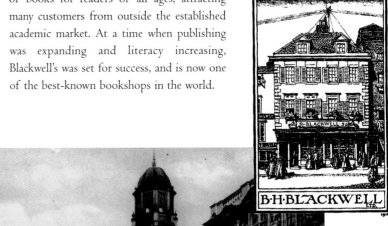

The boundary wall of the Sheldonian Theatre and the classical architecture of the Clarendon Building are conspicuous features in this painting, but the smaller, partially obscured building seen at the end of the street was of considerable significant in the Edwardian era. This was the Indian Institute, whose foundation stone was laid by Edward, Prince of Wales (later to become Emperor of India) in 1883.

In the 1900s it was still true that "the sun never sank on the Empire", and revenue from the Indian subcontinent continued to be crucial to the British economy. The Indian Institute provided somewhere for Indian Civil Service probationers at the University to learn about Indian languages, literature and industry, and a source of information for visiting Indian students wanting to know more about the West. Numbers of students increased in 1908, when they were exempted from examinations in Latin and Greek.

An awning protects books in the window of Blackwell's bookshop from the afternoon sun. Founded in 1879 by Benjamin Henry Blackwell, by the turn of the twentieth century the business had already expanded into properties adjoining the original shop at 50 Broad Street. It now stocked a wide range of books for readers of all ages, attracting many customers from outside the established academic market. At a time when publishing was expanding and literacy increasing, Blackwell's was set for success, and is now one of the best-known bookshops in the world.

NORTH SIDE OF BROAD ST. OXFORD.

Oxford, Sheldonian Theatre

PLATE 33

ALL SAINTS' CHURCH, FROM TURL STREET

The 153-foot steepled tower of All Saints is a fine contribution to the Oxford skyline.

This view of All Saints' Church does not do justice to the classical building that contributes so much to the beauty of Oxford High Street. All Saints was built in the early eighteenth century on the site at the south end of Turl Street of an earlier church. It followed a design by Dr Aldrich, Dean of Christ Church.

Until 1896 the Mayor and Corporation of Oxford had attended St Martin's Church at nearby Carfax. When that building had to be demolished for road widening to accommodate increasing traffic, the civic responsibility passed to All Saints. In 1971 the church was declared redundant, and it is now the library for Lincoln College.

The woman with the basket may be on her way home from the nearby Covered Market. Its stalls stocked a wide variety of fresh produce to meet the demands of townspeople and of chefs from the colleges and local eating establishments. One such hostelry, the ancient Mitre Inn, which stands across the way from All Saints, continues as a thriving restaurant today.

THE MITRE HOTEL, OXFORD.

THIS well-known Hotel, which is situated in the centre of the finest street in Europe, and within a short distance of the river, has been recently enlarged and much improved. While the traditional antiquity of the building has been carefully preserved, visitors will find in it all the refined comforts of a **Modern High-Class Hotel.** During the summer months it is greatly patronised by boating parties. The **"Mitre"** is likewise celebrated as one of the most economical first-class Hotels in the United Kingdom.

DINING, DRAWING, READING, AND SMOKING ROOMS. TEA AND LOUNGE ROOM.
ELECTRIC LIGHT. BILLIARDS. GOOD STABLING.
A Night Porter in attendance.

The Tariff, and an interesting Pamphlet touching upon the traditions of this hostelry, entitled "*Round about 'The Mitre' at Oxford,*" can be obtained post free on application to

MISS K. THORNTON, Manageress.

Oxford, The Turl

PLATE 34

TRINITY COLLEGE

Although set back from the street, Trinity College's chapel was clearly visible to passers-by.

In the 1900s, the remains of an old orchard stood between the college gates on Broad Street and this attractive creeper-covered chapel. Although there are now fewer trees here, the approach to this attractive building still has a very spacious feeling. Built in the late seventeenth century, the chapel is noteworthy both as the first non-Gothic, classical chapel to be built in an Oxford college and for its superb carvings by Grinling Gibbons.

Trinity has large wrought-iron gates (which feature in Fulleylove's Plate 50) at its entrances, rather than the stone gateways and heavy wooden gates of many other colleges, so it has always been possible to enjoy views of the attractive college buildings and extensive grounds from both the Broad Street and Parks Road entrances. According to legend, the Broad Street gates would not be opened until a Stuart sat again on the throne of England, pedestrians being required to enter through an undistinguished gateway alongside. The legend's creator would be disappointed to discover that there is now a drive leading through the gateway.

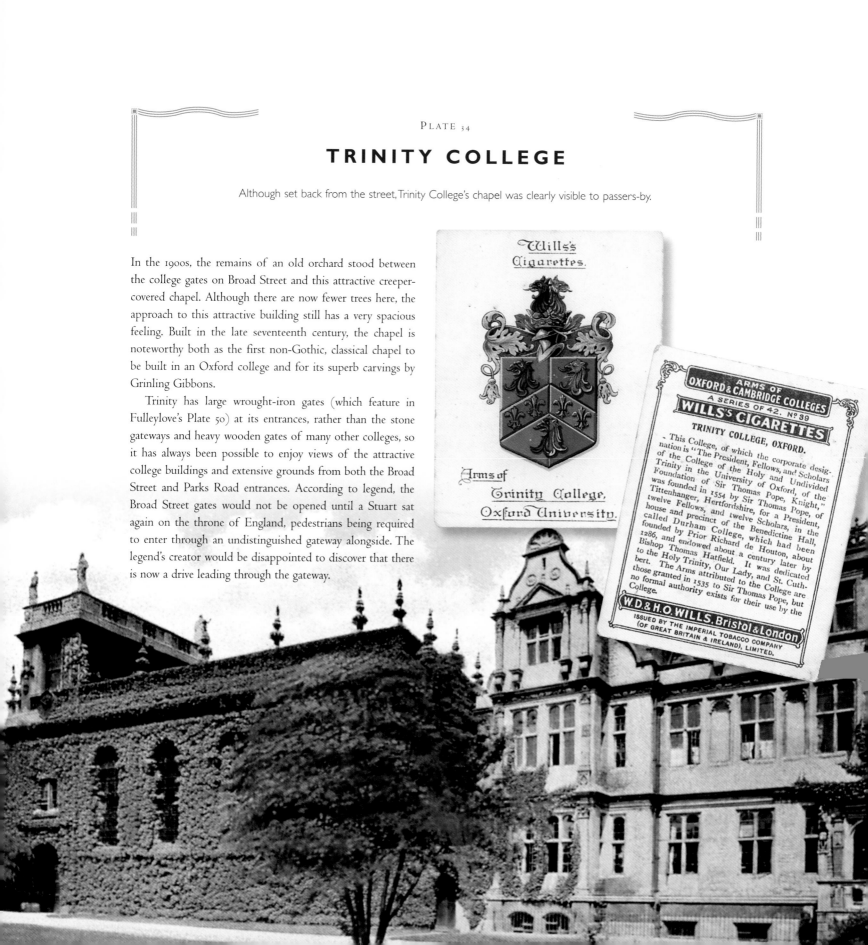

Wills's
Cigarettes.

Arms of
Trinity College,
Oxford University.

ARMS OF
OXFORD & CAMBRIDGE COLLEGES
A SERIES OF 42. Nº 39
WILLS'S CIGARETTES
TRINITY COLLEGE, OXFORD.

This College, of which the corporate designation is "The President, Fellows, and Scholars of the College of the Holy and Undivided Trinity in the University of Oxford, of the Foundation of Sir Thomas Pope, Knight," was founded in 1554 by Sir Thomas Pope, of Tittenhanger, Hertfordshire, for a President, twelve Fellows, and twelve Scholars, in the house and precinct of the Benedictine Hall, called Durham College, which had been founded by Prior Richard de Houton, about 1286, and endowed about a century later by Bishop Thomas Hatfield. It was dedicated to the Holy Trinity, Our Lady, and St. Cuthbert. The Arms attributed to the College are those granted in 1535 to Sir Thomas Pope, but no formal authority exists for their use by the College.

W. D. & H. O. WILLS, Bristol & London
ISSUED BY THE IMPERIAL TOBACCO COMPANY
(OF GREAT BRITAIN & IRELAND), LIMITED.

PLATE 35

INTERIOR OF THE LIBRARY
OF MERTON COLLEGE

The fourteenth-century Upper Library of Merton College is one of the oldest in England.

Merton's library is housed in several parts of the college, and Fulleylove has chosen to paint the oldest part, the Upper Library, which still retains many of its medieval features. As its name suggests, the library was placed on the first floor in order to avoid damp and to obtain maximum light through its narrow lancet windows (replaced by more effective dormer windows in the seventeenth century).

The old oak coffer shown to the left of the staircase harks back to Merton's earliest days, when precious manuscripts were stored in locked chests and valuable books were chained to lecterns.

In the sixteenth century these were replaced by the bookshelves and benches shown in this painting.

Merton College Library houses fascinating collections of papers and memorabilia relating to Max Beerbohm and T.S. Eliot, students at Merton on either side of the Edwardian era. Writer and caricaturist Beerbohm's only novel, *Zuleika Dobson*, a satire on Oxford undergraduate life, was published in 1911, by which time he was already recognised as one of the wittiest minds of his age. American-born Eliot never completed his studies, but went on to receive recognition as one of the twentieth century's finest poets. He was also a dramatist and literary critic.

MERTON COLLEGE LIBRARY,
OXFORD.

PLATE 36

CHRIST CHURCH COLLEGE – TOM QUADRANGLE

This spacious quadrangle reflects the grandiose plans of the founder of Christ Church, Cardinal Thomas Wolsey.

Variously known as the Great Quad, Tom Quad and the Fountain Quad, the dimensions of this quadrangle dwarf all the other courtyards of Oxford. The graceful fountain at its centre was originally created not only as a focus of interest but more importantly to provide water for fire-fighting.

The statue of Mercury shown here was in fact missing at the time Fulleylove painted the scene – it had been removed in 1817 by a wayward student (Edward Stanley, the 14th Earl of Derby, who was later to become a Tory prime minister), and was not replaced until 1928. Fulleylove must therefore have referred to earlier sources for this detail.

The mathematician C.L. Dodgson, better known as Lewis Carroll, had his rooms in the building to the right of the gateway shown here. His classic children's book, now popularly known as *Alice's Adventures in Wonderland*, began as a tale told to entertain the daughters of Dean Liddell during an outing on the river in 1862. This innovative story and its sequel, *Alice Through the Looking-Glass*, proved to be publishing sensations, and both were established bestsellers by 1903.

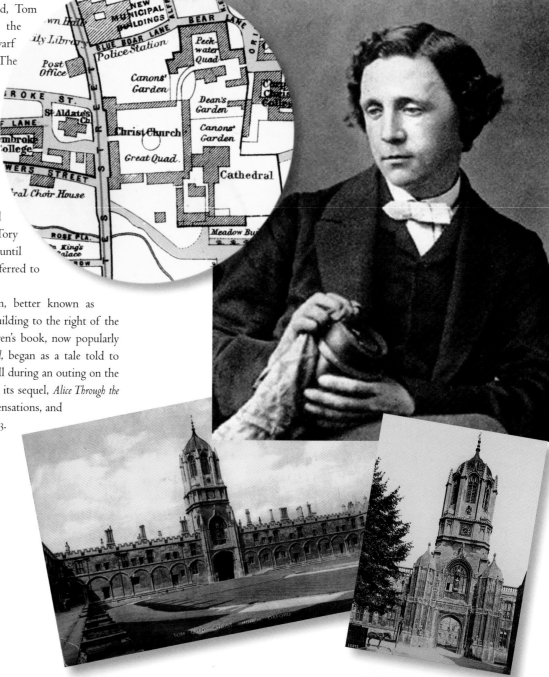

PLATE 37

HOLYWELL CHURCH

The present church was established near a Saxon well reputed
to have healing properties – hence the name "Holywell".

The names of Holywell and St Cross are more or less
interchangeable, although the latter is more commonly used.
Little remains of the original church of St Cross, built outside
the city walls in the late eleventh or early twelfth
centuries – even the tower shown here is a later
addition from about 1270.

The ancient St Cross graveyard was
extended in 1847 when the central city
graveyards became full, and the new Holywell Cemetery was to
become the resting place both of townspeople and a number of
well-known writers, academics and clergy.

In Edwardian times, these included composer John Stainer,
whose works include the magnificent oratorio The Crucifixion.
At his funeral in 1901 the nearby streets were thronged with
mourners wishing to pay their respects. Later in the century,
Kenneth Grahame, author of *The Wind in the Willows*, was buried
here. Published in 1908, his classic Edwardian children's book is
still a much-loved bestseller.

This now-disused cemetery is maintained by a dedicated
group that has created a wildlife haven, a green and quiet corner
in bustling central Oxford.

WILLS'S CIGARETTES

SIR J. STAINER

Love Divine.

Love Divine, all loves excelling,
Joy of Heav'n, to earth come down,
Fix in us Thy humble dwelling,
All Thy faithful mercies crown.

No 25
SECOND SERIES
MUSICAL
CELEBRITIES
WILLS'S
CIGARETTES

SIR JOHN STAINER,
organist and composer,
was born in London, 1840.
He entered St. Paul's Choir,
1847, and succeeded Goss
as cathedral organist, 1872.
In 1880 he received the
Legion of Honour, and a
knighthood in 1888. His
works include many well-
known anthems and church
services, and several can-
tatas, and oratorios, of
which "The Crucifixion" is
the most popular. He died
at Verona, 1901.

ALBUMS FOR THESE PICTURE CARDS CAN BE OBTAINED

AT 1/- EACH FROM ALL TOBACCONISTS.

W.D. & H.O. WILLS
BRISTOL & LONDON
ISSUED BY THE IMPERIAL TOBACCO CO.
(OF GREAT BRITAIN & IRELAND) LT?

THE BATHING SHEDS, OR "PARSONS' PLEASURE"

Members of the University were able to balance academic study with
physical exercise and relaxation at this centuries-old bathing place.

This surprisingly revealing painting of an open-air bathing site
on the Cherwell captures part of University recreational life that
was not usually open to public view.

Parson's Pleasure was reserved for the use of male members of
the University. It was screened off except along the river frontage,
and the willows lining the bank were fitted with platforms for
"plunging". Ladies being transported along the river in punts
or other rivercraft would alight and take an alternative route
overland in order to preserve their modesty.

The evocative name of Parson's Pleasure had little to do with
clergy, and is merely a corruption of Patten's Pleasure, which was
recorded as a bathing place as early as the seventeenth century.

Here it is impossible to distinguish undergraduates from
Fellows — all are simply men, free
to indulge in the delights of bathing
naked in this secluded spot. The
fully-clothed figure may well be
Charlie Cox, keeper of the bathing
sheds for many years, whose name
is commemorated in the University
Parks at Cox's Corner.

PLATE 39

INTERIOR OF THE HALL, MAGDALEN COLLEGE

Magdalen's dining hall was constructed in the late fifteenth century; the fine
carved panels were added during the course of the next century.

At Oxford University the term "Hall" is used for the dining hall of each college, an important location in everyday college life. Edwardian menus were known for their extravagance (possibly influenced by their gourmand monarch), and the meals eaten by the Fellows at High Table would have been no exception. Students sitting at the long refectory tables also benefited from table service, and although their fare might sometimes have been less lavish they still ate very well.

In the late eighteenth century the Hall's original wooden roof was replaced by the vaulted plaster ceiling shown here. However, in 1902, shortly after Fulleylove completed this painting, this plaster ceiling was removed – to be replaced by a brilliant Edwardian reconstruction of the medieval roof!

Many famous people have eaten in this dining hall over the centuries. Magdalen's notable alumni include leaders in many fields of study and from a varied range of professions and areas of public service. The college is also not without its famous Fellows, including author C.S. Lewis who taught here for almost thirty years. What might it have been like to converse with him over dinner?

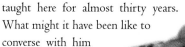

PLATE 40

A "STUDY" IN THE BODLEIAN LIBRARY

These screened-off alcoves in Duke Humfrey's Library are two of four
that originally served as studies for privileged readers.

The Bodleian reading rooms generally maintained a cloister-like silence that was disturbed only by the rustle of papers or the occasional whispered conversation. A lucky few were allocated a place in one of these intimate studies. Here one could focus on one's work or enjoy the view – this study overlooks the Fellows' Garden of Exeter College – or even, perhaps, take an undisturbed nap.

Among the notable books added to the Bodleian's vast collection in the Edwardian era was a dilapidated copy of the First Folio of Shakespeare that had been brought along for examination in 1905. When it was identified as a formerly chained book that had gone missing from the Library more than 150 years earlier. Although funds for new books were limited, £3,000 was quickly raised to buy this precious manuscript and restore it to its rightful home.

Oxford University undergraduates and Fellows must have been a hardy bunch. The Bodleian was well suited to study and quiet contemplation in summertime, but it was bitterly cold and dark in the winter, even during daylight hours. An old steam boiler provided barely adequate heat, and although electric lighting was widely available in the city, ancient statutes designed to limit fire risk meant that electric light was not used in the Old Library until 1928.

PLATE 41

THE TOM QUADRANGLE, CHRIST CHURCH, FROM THE SOUTH ENTRANCE

Architectural details in this view of Tom Quad suggest that Cardinal Wolsey's
original intention was to surround the quadrangle with a cloister.

Wolsey's plans for Tom Quad may never have been completed, but the imposing Great Hall and tower to the right of Fulleylove's painting were an important part of his vision. In recent years the interior of the Hall and the tower's broad stone staircase have become familiar to millions of people from the film versions of J.K. Rowling's *Harry Potter* novels.

Perhaps the figures on the right are here to admire the ornate fan-vaulted roof above this staircase. Or are they on their way to the cathedral? Here its tower and spire are almost dwarfed by the college buildings, a visual reminder that one of the country's smallest cathedrals is found within Oxford's largest college. However modest this spire may appear, it is in proportion with the rest of the building, and is one of the earliest stone spires to be built in England.

Groundsmen working near the fountain are a reminder of the continuing importance of the University to the economy of Oxford. By Edwardian times the railway, gas works, breweries and many academic institutions offered employment opportunities in addition to those at the colleges, but it was a continuing concern that Oxford was in need of non-university employment to support the city's rapidly growing population.

Oxford, Christ Church Dining Hall. (Founded A.D. 1546).

TOM Quad CHRIST C...

W. Matthison

PLATE 42

CORPUS CHRISTI COLLEGE AND MERTON TOWER, FROM CHRIST CHURCH MEADOWS

The Fellows' Building on the south side of Corpus Christi has an unrivalled position overlooking gardens and meadows.

The Fellows of Corpus Christi have long been able to enjoy not only their own formal garden but also a view of the grassy expanse of Christ Church Meadow that lies beyond the college boundaries. Cattle often grazed here, and poplars and willows were among the trees marking the meandering course of the River Cherwell to its confluence with the Isis, better known as the River Thames.

Fulleylove, however, turned his back on this pastoral scene to show the Fellows' Building and part of the old south city wall that separates Corpus Christi from the Meadow. It is interesting to note the "fence" of dahlias growing along the top of the wall. Through the work of the National Dahlia Society,

established in the previous century, these dramatic and colourful flowers, so different from anything found in cottage gardens of the time, had become popular by Edwardian times, especially for competitive showing.

The pinnacle-topped tower of Merton College chapel can be seen to the right. This distinctive T-shaped building was originally intended to be much larger, but plans for an extensive nave were abandoned after a protracted construction programme. Part of Corpus Christi College now stands on this site.

PLATE 43

THE ENTRANCE TO
QUEEN'S COLLEGE FROM LOGIC LANE

Logic Lane – a rather unprepossessing bridleway named after an ancient school of logicians –
opens on to the broad expanse of the High and its many fine college buildings.

In this painting Fulleylove presents a tantalising glimpse of the cupola – with a statue of Queen Caroline, wife of George II – and the entrance to Queen's College. Beyond this gateway lies the College's Front Quad, which has been described by Nikolaus Pevsner as "the grandest piece of classical architecture in Oxford".

By the late nineteenth century undergraduates at Queen's no longer had to make their way to the School Quadrangle – now part of the Bodleian Library – for their exams, but had only to cross the High Street. Here, a short distance to the east, the University's Examination Schools, opened in 1882, were situated; lack of funds meant that the building's fine interior and exterior carvings were not completed until 1909.

Just to the east of Logic Lane was a grocer's shop that, by the turn of the century, was better known as Cooper's "Oxford" Marmalade Shop. In 1874 Frank Cooper's wife had made more marmalade than the family could use, and Cooper sold the excess in his shop. Made to a secret recipe, the preserve proved so popular that the Coopers went on to specialise in its production. In 1900 new regulations forced them to move their production to a new factory near the station, and the company continued to grow. The Cooper's shop remained on the High Street until just after the First World War.

Wills's Cigarettes.

Arms of
Queen's College.
Oxford University.

OXFORD
HOME-MADE
SEVILLE MARMALADE.
WARRANTED PURE
PREPARED ONLY BY
FRANK COOPER.
83 & 84 HIGH ST. OXFORD.

RECOMMENDED BY THE MEDICAL PROFESSION
FOR ITS PURITY AND FINE FLAVOUR.

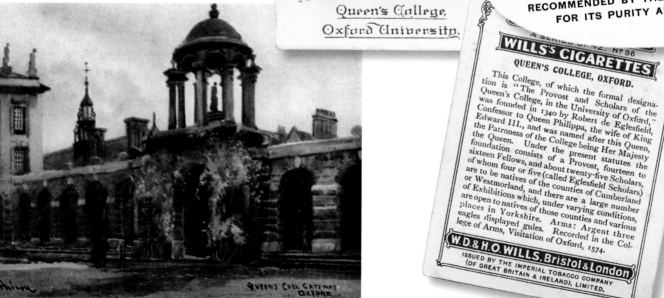

A SERIES OF 42. Nº 36
WILLS'S CIGARETTES
QUEEN'S COLLEGE, OXFORD.
This College, of which the formal designation is "The Provost and Scholars of the Queen's College, in the University of Oxford," was founded in 1340 by Robert de Eglesfield, Confessor to Queen Philippa, the wife of King Edward III, and was named after this Queen, the Patroness of the College being Her Majesty the Queen. Under the present statutes the foundation consists of a Provost, fourteen to sixteen Fellows, and about twenty-five Scholars, of whom four or five (called Eglesfield Scholars) are to be natives of the counties of Cumberland or Westmorland, and there are a large number of Exhibitions which, under varying conditions, are open to natives of those counties and various places in Yorkshire. Arms: Argent three eagles displayed gules. Recorded in the College of Arms, Visitation of Oxford, 1574.
W.D. & H.O. WILLS, Bristol & London
ISSUED BY THE IMPERIAL TOBACCO COMPANY
(OF GREAT BRITAIN & IRELAND), LIMITED.

QUEENS COLL GATEWAY
OXFORD

PLATE 44

EXETER COLLEGE CHAPEL, FROM SHIP STREET

The soaring spire of Exeter College, designed by Victorian architect George Gilbert Scott
in the mid 1800s, is an unmistakable part of the Oxford skyline.

ARMS OF OXFORD & CAMBRIDGE COLLEGES

A SERIES OF 42. Nº 26

WILL'S'S CIGARETTES

EXETER COLLEGE, OXFORD.

Exeter College dates back to 1314, when it was founded by Walter of Stapeldon, Bishop of Exeter, Lord High Treasurer of England, and Secretary of State to King Edward II., and it was at first known as Stapeldon Hall. But in 1404 another Bishop of Exeter—Edmund Stafford—added two Fellowships to the foundation, and the name was thenceforward changed to Exeter College. In 1565, under a Charter granted by Queen Elizabeth, the foundation was enlarged by Sir William Petre. Of the twenty-one Foundation Scholarships, eight ("Stapeldon" Scholarships) are limited to those born or educated within the old limits of the Diocese of Exeter, and one (King Charles I. Scholarship) to those born or educated in the Channel Islands. The keys on the bordure round the shield are taken from the Arms of the See of Exeter.

W.D.&H.O.WILLS, Bristol & London

ISSUED BY THE IMPERIAL TOBACCO COMPANY
(OF GREAT BRITAIN & IRELAND), LIMITED.

This quiet scene in Ship Street must have been a complete contrast to that only a stone's throw away on Cornmarket, one of the city's busiest streets. As a result of growing prosperity in Edwardian times, Cornmarket had become the heart of shopping in Oxford, closely followed by the Covered Market for those seeking provisions.

Jesus College, whose boundary walls can be seen on the right, had a growing number of students, and in 1909 built much-needed student accommodation above a row of shops on the opposite side of Ship Street. In doing this, the college broke away from the model of the old academic halls with students living and studying in the same place.

The focus of this painting is the spire of Exeter College Chapel, whose ornate interior features glittering mosaics, rich stained glass and a tapestry designed by Edward Burne Jones and manufactured by William Morris, both former Exeter students. The décor is said to communicate both "the transcendence and the close intimacy of God", and perhaps it was here that Geoffrey Fisher, an undergraduate in the early twentieth century and later Archbishop of Canterbury, discovered something of his vocation.

PLATE 45

ENTRANCE TO THE DIVINITY SCHOOL

This rather inauspicious hallway leads into one of the most awe-inspiring rooms in Oxford.

It seems strange that this lobby, rather than the beautifully constructed Divinity School itself, has been chosen as the subject of this painting. Through the doors on the right is the first purpose-built lecture room of the University – a room with a breathtaking fan-vaulted ceiling dating from the fifteenth century that Nikolaus Pevsner described as "one of the marvels of Oxford". However, perhaps Fulleylove wanted to arouse our curiosity: to what ceremony is the Vice-Chancellor following the Bedel (the archaic Oxford spelling of "beadle" or town officer charged with the keeping of order) carrying the silver mace?

By the early 1900s the Divinity School – part of the great Schools Quadrangle – was no longer used for examinations or regular lectures. However, this ancient building's many other functions did then include the display of prized possessions from the Bodleian, and it had a role in the annual Encaenia ceremony. While the University dignitaries made their way to the Sheldonian Theatre, those who were to receive honorary degrees waited in the Divinity School and signed their names in the Honorary Degrees Book. Then a Bedel, perhaps the one shown in this painting, would escort them to the Sheldonian Theatre to receive their award.

PLATE 46

THE RIVER ISIS

College barges on the Isis (as the Thames is known in Oxford)
line the banks of Christ Church Meadow to the south of Folly Bridge.

Rowing was an established Oxford sport by the turn of the twentieth century. The University boathouse stood on the west bank of the Isis, but individual colleges did not have their own boathouses. Instead, many colleges had purchased barges, mostly from the London livery companies, which were moored along the opposite riverbank. These were used as club and changing rooms, and also provided college members with excellent viewpoints of the river during races such as Torpids, Eights, and the aptly named Bumping Races or Bumps.

The barges were moored alongside Christ Church Meadow and were moved up- or downriver to show the position of the colleges at the end of Eights. They were easy to identify as each craft was painted in the colours of its college – here Fulleylove focuses on the stately gold and white Magdalen College barge.

A stroll on the other side of the river could sometimes be a hazardous pursuit. At first, those coaching a crew would run along the towpath, but around the turn of the century many acquired bicycles and megaphones, and it was not uncommon for walkers to encounter a distracted speeding cyclist trying hard to keep up with his crew.

PLATE 47

THE SHELDONIAN THEATRE AND OLD CLARENDON BUILDINGS

These important buildings lie just north of the Old Schools Quadrangle and the Bodleian Library.

Surrounded on three sides by the imposing architecture of the Sheldonian Theatre to the west, the Clarendon Building to the north and the Bodleian Library to the south, the area behind these railings is known as the Front Quad. Whenever University dignitaries process across the Quad into the Sheldonian on ceremonial occasions, crowds throng on the nearby pavements to watch. This is also where undergraduates gather on degree days while waiting to be summoned to receive their degrees.

In 1899 an archaeological excavation revealed a postern of the old medieval city wall lying close to the Clarendon Building beneath the Front Quad. This discovery was of great interest to local historians as it confirmed the long suspected location of more of the city's ancient fortifications.

Previously the home of Oxford University Press, by the early twentieth century the Clarendon Building was a multi-purpose building housing the University Registry, the Secretaries of the Curators of the Chest (handling University finances), and several other delegacies and committees. These included the Association for the Education of Women (AEW), whose pioneering work was significant in helping women's colleges become established in Oxford in the late nineteenth century. At a time when suffragettes were demanding the vote, the AEW was pressing for women to be admitted to the male bastion of the University – something that finally happened in 1920.

PLATE 48

JESUS COLLEGE

Founded in 1571, Jesus College is the only Oxford college to date from the Elizabethan period.

Jesus College was founded as a result of the generosity of a treasurer of St David's Cathedral, and it has maintained an association with Wales and Welsh students ever since. The College has a specialist Celtic library and the only chair in Celtic at an English university – the first Professor of Celtic, John Rhys, was at Jesus from the late nineteenth century until 1915.

Among those studying at Jesus in the early twentieth century was T.E. Lawrence, better known as Lawrence of Arabia, who was an undergraduate from 1907 to 1910. One of his contemporaries was Pixley Seme, one of the college's first two Rhodes Scholars. This Zulu chief and politician went on to become one of the co-founders of the African National Congress.

Fulleylove's painting shows two Fellows engaged in debate in the Front Quadrangle. Most of the buildings shown here had been altered or added to since their construction, so Fulleylove may have chosen this view in order to show the original Georgian canopy over the Principal's door.

Wills's Cigarettes.

Arms of Jesus College, Oxford University.

ARMS OF
OXFORD & CAMBRIDGE COLLEGES
A SERIES OF 42. Nº 28
WILLS'S CIGARETTES

JESUS COLLEGE, OXFORD.

This College, which in many respects is essentially Welsh, was founded in the year 1571 by Queen Elizabeth, and the hereditary Visitors of the College are the Earls of Pembroke. A certain Hugh Price, Doctor of Laws, contributed largely to the building, and though the College has no officially recognized claim to Armorial Bearings, the Arms of the aforesaid Dr. Hugh Price are made use of. For nearly all the Fellowships, and for most of the Scholarships the preference is given to natives of Wales or Monmouthshire, though King Charles I.'s foundation is restricted to candidates from the Channel Islands—either born there or educated at Victoria College, Jersey, or Elizabeth College, Guernsey.

W. D. & H. O. WILLS, Bristol & London
ISSUED BY THE IMPERIAL TOBACCO COMPANY
(OF GREAT BRITAIN & IRELAND), LIMITED.

PLATE 49

FELLOWS' GARDEN, EXETER COLLEGE

Open green spaces such as quadrangles and gardens are a feature of most Oxford University colleges.

Without the distractions of modern technology, life moved at a slower pace when Fulleylove was recording the Oxford scene. Here a group of Fellows are seated under an acacia, maybe relaxing after a game of bowls. Times have certainly changed, and wireless internet access is now possible in many parts of Oxford University, including this peaceful leafy garden. Would one observe such a scene today?

Bishop Heber's tree (see Plate 3) can be seen between the aged acacia tree and the dome of the Radcliffe Library. This grew at the south-east corner of an embankment overlooking Radcliffe Square. From here the view one could see was often referred to as "the focus of the University": a panorama of Oxford in microcosm, with undergraduates hurrying between lectures, a lad from the Covered Market pushing a laden cart to make a delivery to a college kitchen, and visitors to the city admiring the spectacular architecture on every side of the square.

Oxford, Exeter College. (Founded A.D. ...

PLATE 50

IN TRINITY COLLEGE GARDENS

Trinity remains one of the smallest Oxford colleges, yet its extensive
and varied gardens have long been a match for many larger colleges.

When American novelist Henry James described Oxford college gardens as green retreats "from the restless outer world … places to lie down on the grass for ever, in the happy faith that life is all a vast old English garden and time an endless summer afternoon", he might well have been thinking of those at Trinity College.

Not only does Trinity have several quadrangles, including one partly created by Christopher Wren; there are also separate gardens for fellows and graduates, a glade of trees known as The Wilderness, and an extensive area of lawns to the east of the college buildings. These were well established by the 1900s, and were enjoyed both by members of the college and by those who passed the wrought-iron gates shown in this painting and could look in at this quintessentially English scene.

Fulleylove, in contrast with his more familiar landscapes, here chose to capture an intimate garden. This woman resting in the shade of an ancient tree must have been a visitor to Trinity College; although women were able to study in Oxford at this time, the University had not yet admitted female students to full membership.

Trinity College, Lime Walk.

Oxford.

PLATE 51

THE FELLOWS' GARDEN, MERTON COLLEGE

This terrace at the south of the Fellows' Garden runs along part of Oxford's old city walls.

The Fellows' Garden at Merton was, like the quads and gardens of most Oxford colleges, hidden away behind college walls. However, anyone relaxing in this garden could choose to climb onto the terrace walk, from where it was possible to see outside the college grounds. From this viewpoint a magnificent vista opened up which included Merton Field, Broad Walk, and out across Christ Church Meadow.

As well as the grand avenue of lime trees on the left, the garden boasted an ancient sycamore that at the time of this painting was already two hundred years old. It is said that this fine tree later became a favourite of the nature-loving J.R.R. Tolkien, who was appointed Merton Professor of English in 1945. Some have also speculated that it was while walking along the terraced medieval walls that he found inspiration for some of the many battlements described in *The Lord of the Rings*.

Merton College

Circ: 1290–1400.
Circ: 1400–1500.
Circ: 1588–1631.
19th & 20th Cent.

1. Entrance Gateway. 4. Treasury.
2. Patey's Quad. 5. Queen's Room.
3. Sacristy. 6. Old Warden's Lodgings.

Oxford, Merton College, St Alban's Quad, (Founded 1264)

PLATE 52

THE LIBRARY, ORIEL COLLEGE

The senior library at Oriel had to make room for an
additional collection of books early in the twentieth century.

When Oriel College united with the adjoining St Mary Hall
in 1902, Oriel's already significant book collection became even
larger.

The senior library had been constructed in the late eighteenth
century to accommodate a library that had recently doubled
in size as the result of a generous bequest. Its construction
completed a programme that transformed a garden into what is
known as the Back or Second Quad. The ornate, neo-classical
library is on the first floor, above the common room – the first
purpose-built common room in an Oxford college.

The two gardeners shown here are a reminder of the many
non-academic staff required for the smooth running and
upkeep of the colleges. Students, staff and ancient buildings all
demanded considerable attention. By
the turn of the century most University
colleges were connected to an electricity
supply, thus reducing the need to attend
to gas lights, and gradually new labour-
saving devices would begin to lessen the
load of college domestic staff.

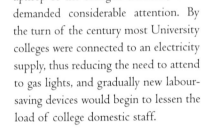

PLATE 53

MAGDALEN COLLEGE TOWER, FROM THE MEADOWS

Magdalen's location outside the old city walls gave the college a lasting air of spaciousness.

One could be forgiven for thinking that Magdalen College has a rural location. Outside the city walls, the college has been able to expand, something that few city centre colleges could contemplate, and its extensive grounds provide a breathing space away from the bustle of the city. In this painting, Magdalen Tower is shown surrounded by various groups of trees including black poplars – now an extremely rare species in Britain – and elms, found mostly in "The Grove" or deer park.

A small herd of fallow deer has been kept at Magdalen since the early eighteenth century, and venison is a popular dish on the college menu. There are tales of undergraduates feeding the deer with sugar cubes dipped in port wine to get them drunk. Perhaps this student prank began in Edwardian times, following the recent introduction of sugar in cubes.

Magdalen's extensive grounds include secluded footpaths beside the water meadows where rare snakeshead fritillaries flower each spring. Addison's Walk, a path between two branches of the Cherwell, has long been a popular spot with members of the college and townspeople. The quest for fitness that became popular in the Edwardian era no doubt brought increased numbers of walkers to this peaceful place.

Oxford, Magdalen College, Deer Park

PLATE 54

THE CLOISTERS, NEW COLLEGE

The great west window of New College Chapel, painted from designs made
by Sir Joshua Reynolds, can be seen above the east end of the cloisters.

These cloisters were originally intended for processions on feast days, burials and "academic meditation", thus reflecting the monastic tradition of the college. It must have been a peaceful place for the gardeners hard at work in this painting, or perhaps they are being entertained by the sound of the college choir practising in the chapel.

New College is one of three Oxford colleges with a school, the others being Christ Church and Magdalen. The New College School was originally established for choristers in 1379, but by the seventeenth century there were a significant number of other schoolboys or "commoners". As a result

of further growth, including taking on the choirboys from the Queen's College, the school outgrew its premises, and in 1903 it moved to a new site a few minutes' walk from New College.

The college has long been famous for its choristers, but in the Edwardian era it also became renowned for its oarsmen. By the beginning of the twentieth century they had established themselves as a force to be reckoned with, despite having to change crews each year when students completed their studies. The New College eight was among the top three on the river for more than twenty years from 1883 to 1906. As the college is some distance from the river, perhaps making the daily journey to practice gave them an extra edge.

NEW COLLEGE CLOISTERS, OXFORD.

PLATE 55

BROAD STREET, LOOKING WEST

This aptly named street is less than half the length of the High Street, but it is twice as wide.

There have been head-and-shoulder busts on the enclosing wall of the Sheldonian Theatre since it was completed in 1668. No one seems quite sure who they represent, although in his 1911 Oxford novel *Zuleika Dobson* Max Beerbohm called them the "Emperors", and observed that "they are by American visitors frequently mistaken for the Twelve Apostles". It is the former name that has stuck.

On both sides of Broad Street are figures with bicycles. By the turn of the twentieth century the bicycle was no longer merely a plaything of the rich; ever-falling prices made them more widely accessible to the middle and lower middle classes. The bicycle also gained popularity with University staff and students, and its convenience in Oxford's crowded narrow streets means it is just as popular today as it was a hundred years ago.

However, another popular form of transport was soon to go into decline – the horse-drawn hansom cab. The small dark shape in the middle distance is probably the hansom cab shelter that could be found in the centre of Broad Street until shortly after the end of Edward VII's reign. The time of the motor car had come, and less than twenty years later the centre of Broad Street was given over to parked cars.

PLATE 56

THE HIGH STREET, LOOKING EAST

"Town" and "gown" rub shoulders in the busy High Street close to the crossroads at Carfax.

There were many changes in central Oxford during the years around the turn of the twentieth century. Increasing levels of traffic at the Carfax crossroads, close to where Fulleylove painted this scene, made it necessary to demolish much of St Martin's Church in 1896. Only the church tower, now known as Carfax Tower, was left standing. The following year there was much excitement when the Prince of Wales (soon to become King Edward VII) visited the city to open the new Town Hall just to the south of Carfax.

At the centre of Oxford the focus was not on the University but on commerce. Four "avenues" on the north side of the High led to the Covered Market, and in the 1900s the wide range of shops and businesses on both sides of the street included a draper, tobacconist, bootmaker, stationer and bank. There were also two businesses that continue to thrive today: Gills, one of the oldest ironmongers in the country, dating from the mid-sixteenth century, and the ancient Mitre Inn, shown to the left of this painting.

Even amidst the hustle and bustle it must have been difficult to ignore some of the striking architecture further to the west along the High – the soaring spires of All Saints Church and the University Church of St Mary the Virgin, and part of the "battlements" of All Souls.

TOWN HALL, OXFORD.

High St and Carfax OXFORD.

PLATE 57

THE BOTANIC GARDEN

The grounds of this beautifully maintained garden were a popular place
to "promenade", to find a spot to rest, or to seek inspiration.

In the early years of the twentieth century there was a widespread renewal of interest in gardens and garden design, inspired by pioneers like the plantswoman Gertrude Jekyll and the architect-designer Edwin Lutyens. For the keen horticulturalist, Oxford's Botanic Garden would have been the ideal place to visit — for information, inspiration and relaxation.

Developed on the banks of the River Cherwell, this classic seventeenth-century walled garden was built on ground leased from the nearby Magdalen College. It was originally established in 1621 as a physic garden with a collection of medicinal plants and herbs, and trees and plants were arranged in formal patterns.

The garden went through periods of activity and periods of neglect over the centuries and underwent considerable changes during the reign of Queen Victoria. In 1850 its name was changed from "physic" to "botanic", marking a new, broader scope than just medicine — what could plant study also do for the fields of science and industry? In the 1880s much of the garden was rearranged to create the beds and planting that were in place at the start of the twentieth century.

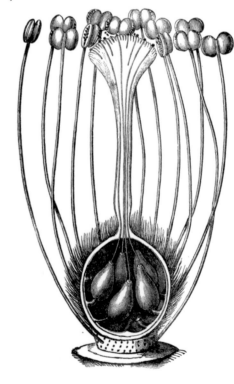

PLATE 58

OXFORD, FROM SOUTH HINKSEY

A view similar to this inspired the poet Matthew Arnold to write in his poem "Thyrsis" of "that sweet city with her dreaming spires …"

Matthew Arnold – a Fellow of Oriel College – was clearly fond of the Oxfordshire countryside, for he included the village of South Hinksey in another poem, "The Scholar Gypsy".

In this painting it is possible to identify the distinctive towers and spires of All Saints Church, the Radcliffe Library, the University Church of St Mary, Tom Tower at Christ Church and, farther to the right, those of the Cathedral and Merton Chapel.

Pedestrians used a causeway – which sometimes flooded – to cross the swampy, low-lying land between South Hinksey and the southern part of the city. From the mid-

nineteenth century there was an additional hazard – the newly constructed railway line from London to Oxford.

In the early twentieth century, visitors glimpsing the city skyline from the train might have been surprised by what awaited them as they approached Oxford station. Here the architecture was mainly industrial and commercial, a stark contrast with that of the ancient churches and college buildings. The railway line ran past a gasometer, the smell of a nearby brewery hung in the air, and just over the road from the station was the recently opened Frank Cooper's marmalade factory.

PLATE 59

OXFORD, FROM HEADINGTON HILL

This bucolic view of the city made Headington a popular destination for Oxford residents' country walks.

It is hard to believe that this rural hillside, possibly what is now South Park, lay within the city bounds. Yet it had become part of Oxford when the municipal boundaries were extended in 1889, and building in the city was expanding rapidly along the lower-lying ground.

The famous elm trees that grew in Magdalen College "Grove" can be seen to the left of the painting. The two spires nearby are those of the Cathedral and the University Church of St Mary, with the Radcliffe dome and "Schools" tower farther to the right. Although the main London Road ran down Headington Hill, the view afforded to travellers was limited as the road ran through a cutting.

The Morrell family of local brewers established a country estate on nearby grazing land in the nineteenth century. Their home, the Italianate Headington Hill Hall, has since then been a military hospital and home to publishing tycoon Robert Maxwell. It is now part of Oxford Brookes University.

L.W.HASLEHUST.

PLATE 60

THE OLD ASHMOLEAN MUSEUM AND SHELDONIAN THEATRE

The Ashmolean can lay claim to be Britain's first official museum, and is one of the oldest public museums in the world.

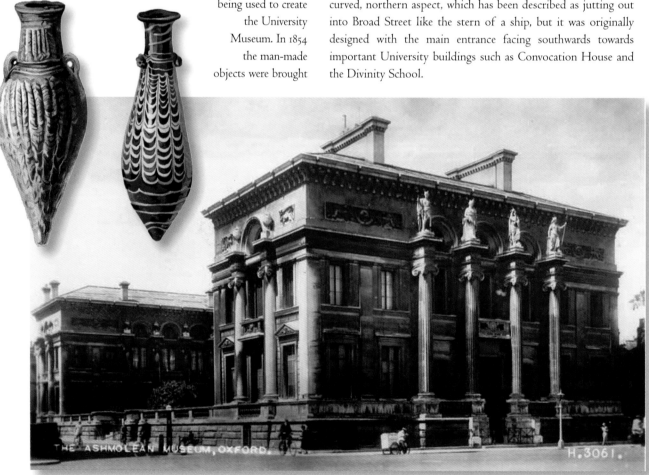

To the left of this painting are the fine, canopied porch and doorway of the original Ashmolean Museum. This was built in the seventeenth century to house the School of Natural History, the first chemical laboratory in England, and the somewhat idiosyncratic Tradescant Collection which was given to the University by Elias Ashmole in 1677.

Over time the collection in the Ashmolean grew, and in the mid-Victorian period it was split into natural and man-made divisions, with the former being used to create the University Museum. In 1854 the man-made objects were brought together with the University's expanding collection of antiquities and works of art in a new neo-classical building in Beaumont Street. Situated opposite the Randolph Hotel, this quickly became a popular attraction in Edwardian times, and its appeal was further enhanced when the collections of the new Ashmolean Museum and the University's art gallery were merged in 1908.

To the right of the painting is part of the south front of the Sheldonian Theatre. Most people are more familiar with its curved, northern aspect, which has been described as jutting out into Broad Street like the stern of a ship, but it was originally designed with the main entrance facing southwards towards important University buildings such as Convocation House and the Divinity School.

THE ASHMOLEAN MUSEUM, OXFORD.

H.3061.

To write the text for *Oxford*, A&C Black introduced one of the few authors of real distinction to the colour book series: Edward Thomas (1878–1917), who was better known as a poet, but who from time to time worked (in his own words) as "a doomed hack" to make ends meet.

Henry W. Nevinson, literary editor of *The News Chronicle* and a champion of "causes", was approached first, but he suggested as a substitute the 25-year-old Thomas, who was already working as a book reviewer for the newspaper. The fee paid for this uncongenial task was £100 for 50,000 words (in fact he wrote 60,000). These were vital funds for Thomas, who was perennially hard up. He had matriculated at Oxford as a non-collegiate student in 1897 and graduated in history in 1900, so he knew his subject well. In spite of his dislike of this sort of work, he did not skimp the task. There are passages of what his biographer R. George Thomas calls his worst "colour book" style, but *Oxford* also contains much humorous and observant writing, including loosely disguised portraits of dons and undergraduates, including Raymond Asquith, F.E. Smith and Hilaire Belloc. *The Studio*, in its review in 1904, accused Thomas of missing the serious side of the subject and having "more than once degenerated into flippancy", and the magazine regretted that more dignified treatment had not been meted out to the alma mater. But it seems to have been used to more solemn texts than Thomas's.

In January 1903 John Fulleylove was offered £100 for 50 illustrations, rather less than A&C Black usually offered – William Matthison, painter of *Cambridge*, for example, was offered the more usual figure of £150. The fee was only for the rights to reproduce, and the list of illustrations printed in the book show that 40 of the 60 had already been sold – the owners are named – while the remaining 20 were still the property of the artist. *The Studio*, in its review, regarded the drawings as "full of charm, though they share the limitations of the 'three-colour process', which is never successful in the interpretation of green".

Oxford was published on 11 December 1903 in a large paper edition limited to 300 copies, to sell at 2 guineas (£2.10) each, bound in white cloth and printed on handmade paper, numbered and signed A&C Black. The publisher's advertisements said that every copy would be signed by the artist, but there is no evidence that this happened. The trade edition was published on 15 December 1903 in the *Twenty Shilling Series*. The edition of 3,200 was bound in blue cloth with designs in gilt on the front and spine.

Oxford was reprinted in 1911, and the text plus 32 of the original 60 illustrations was later issued in the *Popular and New* series in the 1920s. Twelve illustrations with a new text by Joseph E. Morris appeared in the *Beautiful Britain* Series in 1911; and twenty of the illustrations in the Black's *Water-Colour Series* in 1916. Fulleylove's paintings were also much reproduced as postcards by A&C Black themselves as well as the Robert Peel Postcard Company.

Edward Thomas went on to write *Wales* in the *Twenty Shilling Series*. He was killed on the Western Front in 1917 and is commemorated in Poets' Corner in Westminster Abbey. The manuscript of *Oxford* was presented to Lincoln College, Oxford (Thomas's college) in 1918.

A New World of Colour Printing

The late Victorians and Edwardians loved colour, and great strides in printing and ink technology allowed them to have it, breaking free of the limitations of the monotone pages of their parents' generation with their woodcuts and steel engravings. Many of these developments came from Germany, where by the turn of the nineteenth century there was a lucrative industry in colour postcards, greetings cards, and books containing dozens of colour illustrations.

The challenge and promise of colour were quickly taken up in Britain, where presses – especially in London and Edinburgh – started using the latest technology to print colour plates for a range of reference books.

Until the early 1890s, anyone wanting to print a colour image had to design the images in such a way that the different colours, each printed from its own plate, could easily be separated from each other. Many ways were developed to create subtlety in the use of colour, including engraving fine detail into each colour plate, using separate plates for different tones of the same colour, and hand-finishing each plate after it had been printed. Even so, most colour printing in 1900 was fairly crude, and it is clear – especially under the magnifying glass – that the drive for realistic colour still had some way to go.

The best colour printing in 1900, however, was stunning. In the period between 1900 and 1914, before war dried up ink and machinery supplies from Germany to the rest of the world, printing in colour reached a peak not to be reached again until the 1960s.

How did they achieve this quality? It is important to remember that outdoor colour photography as we know it, using colour film to photograph places

Merton and Christ Church, an 1890s photochrome (top right); "Sweet Peas", reproduced by the Andsleigh Direct Colour Process, from *The Process Year Book* 1905–6 (top left); "Dessert", printed from three-colour blocks by Kollien, from *The Process Year Book* 1906–7 (bottom).

The Process of the Future

is the

**Hentschel=
Colourtype Process**

America's Opinion of the
Hentschel-
Colourtype Process.

The American 'Inland Printer'
says :

"The etching of the **Hentschel** Plates is
admirably done.. One thing can be said with
certainty, that if the colour plate makers of
the world could but make colour plates like
Carl Hentschel they would change the whole
style of Illustration, which should, in truth,
be in colour."

THE ONLY
THREE-COLOUR
PROCESS
WHICH GIVES
FACSIMILE AND
ARTISTIC RESULTS.

All the Leading Artists
have testified as to its
excellence.

For further particulars apply to

Carl Hentschel, Ltd.

The Leading and Largest Firm of
Process Engravers in the World.

Undertaking every class of
Process Engraving in Tone,
Line or Colour.

Specimens of their Work can be
seen in all the leading
Illustrated Journals and Magazines.

Head Offices :
182-3-4, Fleet Street, London, E.C.

Carl Hentschel (left) and the original Three Men in a Boat (right) – Carl Hentschel,
George Wingrave and Jerome K. Jerome. Hentschel was a good friend of Jerome's.

It was now possible to photograph flat objects like paintings, or small groups of objects in a studio setting, in colour. And it was possible to use those images, separated into their three component process colours, to print colour images. It was impossible, however, to make colour photographs of the wide outside world, of cities, mountains and crowds of people. Yet once they had a taste of colour postcards and colour pictures in books, those who could afford to buy such relatively expensive luxuries wanted as much colour as they could get.

The images in this book demonstrate the many ways in which Edwardian inventors, photographers and publishers strove to give their customers what they so craved – the real world on the printed page in full colour.

and people, was not invented until the 1930s. However, from about 1890 onwards, several processes for making colour photographs of inanimate objects in a studio setting were well advanced, and Edwardian photographers were amazingly inventive.

One of the greatest pioneers was a German émigré, Carl Hentschel, who in the 1890s patented the Hentschel Colourtype Process and set up his company in London's Fleet Street. Hentschel developed a massive camera which used three colour filters – red, green and blue – to capture simultaneous images of any flat colour original. At the same time, developments such as the halftone screen, allowing colour gradation to be printed as an almost imperceptible regular pattern of different-sized dots onto paper, was enabling photographed images to be transferred to paper, both in black and white and in the new three-colour "process" method.

Cottage at Clifton Hampden
(right), from Oxford from Original
Watercolour Paintings by A.R. Quinton,
Salmon, 1907. The Hentschel
advertisement (above) was printed
in the 1904–5 Process Year Book.
The Chromographoscope (far
right), invented by du Hauron in
1874, was a dual-purpose machine.
It could be used as a camera or as
an additive viewer.

COTTAGE AT CLIFTON HAMPDEN
BERKSHIRE

Sources, Notes and Captions

The images used to complement the paintings come from a wide variety of sources, including books, postcards, museums and libraries. They include photochromes, ephemera, adverts and maps of the period. The photochromes and more than 5,000 others can be seen online at www.ushistoricalarchive.com/photochroms/index.html. The cigarette cards come from a series of 42 cards of Oxford and Cambridge college coats of arms published in 1922. The large coloured numbers refer to the plate numbers.

1 The painting by E.W. Haslehust of the Old Clarendon Building in Broad Street is from *Oxford*, described by F.D. How and published by Blackie and Son Ltd in 1915. The view of Broad Street and Balliol College, painted by William Matthison (lower right) is from *Oxford* by Robert Peel and H.C. Minchin, published by Methuen in 1905. On the left, the Clarendon Building features in *Ackermann's Oxford*, originally published in 1814.

2 Clockwise from the top right, the postcard of the Clarendon Press and Sheldonian Theatre in 1900 is from the Valentine Collection, and can be found on *The Oxford Explorer*, published by Hugo Brown. "The Interior of the Sheldonian Theatre" was published by George Davis between 1902 and 1918, also from *The Oxford Explorer*. "The Spires of Oxford" is a painting by William Matthison from Peel and Minchin's *Oxford*.

3 The portrait of Bishop Heber is accompanied by a map showing Exeter College and Gardens, from the cover to *Alden's Oxford Guide* published in 1916. The chromolithograph of the horse chestnut leaf, flower and fruit by W.H.J. Boot is from Vol. 1 of *Familiar Trees* by G.S. Boulger, published by Cassell and Co. in 1906.

4 The painting on the left of St Edmunds Hall by Matthison is from Peel and Minchin's *Oxford*; the view on the right comes from *Pictures in Colour of Oxford* by Alfred Savage, published by Jarrold & Sons around 1900. Many of the pictures in this publication were subsequently used for postcard reproductions.

5 Two images of St Mary's Porch, the one on the right by Alfred Savage from *Pictures in Colour of Oxford*; the middle one by Matthison from Peel and Minchin's *Oxford*. The view of St Mary's Tower is from *100 Views of Oxford*, published by Penrose and Palmer around 1925.

6 The two views of Iffley Church are from a 1911 postcard published by Frith, included in *The Oxford Explorer*, and from *Pictures in Colour of Oxford*. The painting on the right is by E.W. Haslehust, from his *Oxford*.

7 The bottom view of Christ Church College is by Alfred Savage from *Pictures in Colour of Oxford*. On the right is a postcard of Tom Tower, Christ Church, reproduced as an advertisement of the original A&C Black title on which this book is based.

8 Top right is St Giles and The Martyrs' Memorial by William Matthison from Peel and Minchin's *Oxford*. The drawing by A. Brunet-Debaines of the entrance to St John's College (bottom right) is from *Oxford* by Andrew Lang, published by Seeley and Co. in 1906. The advertisement for the Randolph Hotel features in *Near Oxford* by Rev. H.T. Inman, published by Aldman & Co. in 1904.

9 Matthison's painting of Christ Church Cathedral (bottom left) is from Peel and Minchin's *Oxford*. The detail is from a carving of the Shrine of St Frideswide and the stained glass is from the Latin Chapel. The painting (right) of the Latin Chapel is from Peel and Minchin's *Oxford*.

10 The image of Sadler's balloon is from a contemporary engraving. The 1906 postcard (bottom right) of St Peters-in-the-East and the postcard of its Norman doorway were both published by Frith, and can be found on *The Oxford Explorer*. Yoshio Markino is the Japanese-born artist of the view of St Peters-in-the-East, which comes from Hugh de Sélincourt's *Oxford from Within*, published by Chatto and Windus in 1910.

11 The view (right) of University College Chapel is from a Stengel & Co. postcard of 1905, reproduced on *The Oxford Explorer*. University College (left) is from *Pictures in Colour of Oxford* by Alfred Savage, published by Slater & Rose c.1910. The inset shows Clement Attlee.

12 The cover, and the illustration of Merton's Mob Quad, come from *Merton College, Oxford* by H. J. White, published by J.M. Dent & Co. in 1906.

13 The central image of Cecil Rhodes is from *Edward VII: His Life and Times*, Vol. 2, published by The Amalgamated Press in 1910. On the left, Oriel College painted by Yoshio Markino is from *Oxford from Within*.

14 On the right, the map of Grove Street comes from *Alden's Oxford Guide*. The view of Grove Street on the right is from *Oxford from Within*. The postcard was published by Penrose, and comes from *The Oxford Explorer*. The "real photograph" postcard of Grove Street at the top is dated 1904.

15 The photograph of the City Wall from New College Garden is from Penrose & Palmer's *100 Views of Oxford*, c.1900. The painting by Matthison is from Peel and Minchin's *Oxford*. *The New College* in The College Monographs series was written by A.O. Prickard and published by J.M. Dent in 1906.

16 The interior view of the Bodleian Library (bottom left) is from a 1902 Frith postcard included on *The Oxford Explorer*. The top image is from *Old England: A Pictorial Museum of Regal, Ecclesiastical, Municipal, Baronial, and Popular Antiquities*, Vol. 2, by Charles Knight and published by J. Sangster & Co. c.1860. Bottom right is a painting by Matthison from Peel and Minchin's *Oxford*.

17 The coins are a 1903 sixpence (obverse), a 1903 sixpence (reverse) and a 1910 shilling. The main image is Alfred Savage's view of All Souls' College from *Pictures in Colour of Oxford*.

18 The principal image of Magdalen College Cloisters and Founders Tower is from *Pictures in Colour of Oxford*. The inset (right) of the Cloisters is from *The Oxford Explorer*.

19 The postcard on the right, of St John's College Gardens, is from *The Oxford Explorer*. Bottom left is St Johns College from *Pictures in Colour of Oxford*.

20 The painting by E.W. Haslehust (right) of the Botanic Gardens and Magdalen Tower is from his *Oxford*. Bottom left is a postcard of the Botanic Gardens, c.1940, from *The Oxford Explorer*. The inset of "Hardy Water Lilies" is from Vol. 6 of *Thompson's Gardener's Assistant* by Robert Thompson and William Watson, published by Gresham in 1906. "The Speckled Wood Butterfly" comes from *Butterflies of the British Isles* by Richard South, in The Wayside and Woodland Series published by Frederick Warne in 1906.

21 On the right, the picture of Magdalen Tower is from *100 Views of Oxford*. Bottom left is a 1905 postcard showing the Magdalen Choir, entitled "May Morning on Magdalen Tower".

22 Matthison painted the view of All Souls' College with St Mary's behind for Peel and Minchin's *Oxford*. The 1911 postcard view of All Souls' from the Radcliffe Camera comes from *The Oxford Explorer*. In the centre, the watercolour painting of the High Street is by A.R. Quinton.

23 The 1910 photograph of the ceremony conferring Honorary Degrees is from *The Oxford Explorer*. The sketch by Fred Richards, entitled "Greek and Latin Essay Rostrum", comes from *Oxford: A Sketchbook*, published by A&C Black in 1913. On the right is an 1890 photochrome of the Sheldonian Theatre.

24 The image of Corpus Christi College (bottom left) is from *Pictures in Colour of Oxford*. In the centre is a painting by J.H. Lorimer of Corpus Christi College, which forms the title page of the 1906 edition of *Oxford* by Andrew Lang.

25 Both postcards, from different perspectives, of Christ Church's Peckwater Quadrangle are by Frith, and are included on *The Oxford Explorer*. The painting of the same quad is by William Matthison from Peel and Minchin's *Oxford*.

26 Three very different presentations of the same subject: Yoshio Markino's version of the Radcliffe Camera comes from *Oxford from Within*; The Radcliffe by A. Brunet-Debaines is in Lang's *Oxford*; Radcliffe Camera and All Souls, painted by William Matthison, is from Peel and Minchin's *Oxford*. The illustration by H.E. Dresser of "The Mallard, or Wild Duck", is from *Birds of Britain* by J. Lewis Bonhote, published by A&C Black in 1907.

27 The main image, of Hertford College, is from *Pictures in Colour of Oxford*.

28 The left and middle views of Christ Church Cathedral are both by Matthison, from Peel and Minchin's *Oxford*. To the right is Christ Church Cathedral from *Pictures in Colour of Oxford*.

29 The 1907 postcard, Magdalen Botanical Gardens from the Cherwell (bottom right), is from *The Oxford Explorer*. The A.R. Quinton painting (bottom left) is of Magdalen College and Bridge, Oxford. The 1906 postcard (top right) of Punting on the Cherwell is by Frith, and can be found on *The Oxford Explorer*. The inset of "The Canna Lily" is from *Thompson's Gardener's Assistant*, Vol. 2.

30 The Radcliffe Library Interior (bottom right) was painted by Matthison for Peel and Minchin's *Oxford*. The 1903 postcard of Radcliffe Library (bottom left) is from the "Oxford Artist Series".

31 The illustration by Sir John Tenniel of Alice and the sheep was first published in *Through the Looking-Glass and What Alice Found There* in 1872. The 1906 Frith postcard on the right, of Bishop King's House, is included on *The Oxford Explorer*. The map of Bishop King's "Palace", as it was earlier known, is from *Alden's Oxford Guide*.

32 The upper photograph of Blackwell's in Broad Street dates from about 1920. The image on the left, of the north side of Broad Street in the 1930s, is from *The Oxford Explorer*. The 1910 advertisement for Blackwell's is reproduced in *Adventurers All* by Rita Ricketts, published by Blackwell's in 1988. The 1910 Frith postcard (bottom right) of the Sheldonian comes from *The Oxford Explorer*.

33 The 1911 Frith postcard of All Saints' Church along Turl Street is included on *The Oxford Explorer*. The advertisement for the Mitre Hotel comes from *Alden's Oxford Guide*. Yoshio Markino painted the view of The Turl on the left; it is reproduced in Hugh de Sélincourt's *Oxford from Within*.

34 The main picture of Trinity College and Presidents House is from *Pictures in Colour of Oxford*.

35 On the left, William Matthison's painting of Merton College Library is from Peel and Minchin's *Oxford*. Ernest Stamp drew Merton Library, from Lang's *Oxford* (centre). On the right is a first edition of *Zuleika Dobson* by Max Beerbohm.

36 The portrait of Lewis Carroll is by his friend Oscar Gustave Rejlander, a pioneering Victorian art photographer. The map showing Christ Church College is from *Alden's Guide to Oxford*. The 1900 Penrose postcard of Tom Quad (bottom left) is from *The Oxford Explorer*. Bottom right is an 1890s photochrome of Tom Tower.

37 The postcard featuring "Love Divine", a hymn written by John Stainer, was published by E.A. Schwerdtieger, c.1914. The 1910 postcard of St Cross village showing Holywell Church comes from *The Oxford Explorer*.

38 The central painting by Lancelot Speed is titled "Parson's Pleasure", and comes from *Oxford* by Andrew Lang. Thomas Eakin's painting of "The Swimming Hole", painted in 1885, includes himself as one of the nude figures. The leaves of the weeping willow are from *Familiar Trees*, Vol. 3, Cassell, 1906.

39 "Entrées" (left) and Savarin d'Abricots (right) come from Vol. 3 of *The Book of the Home: A Comprehensive Guide on All Matters Pertaining to the Household* by Mrs C.E. Humphrey (also known as "Madge" of Truth), Gresham Publishing Co., c.1910.

40 The advertisement of the Tercentenary of the Bodleian Library, celebrated in 1902, comes from *Alden's Oxford Guide*. Duke Humfrey's Library (left) forms part of the Bodleian Library; the image comes from *The Oxford Explorer*. The Ernest Stamp sketch, "In the Bodleian", is in Lang's *Oxford*.

41 The view on the right of Christ Church Dining Hall in 1911 is from *The Oxford Explorer*. Bottom left is Christ Church Tom Quad by William Matthison, from Peel and Minchin's *Oxford*. The wrought iron barrow is from *Thompson's Gardener's Assistant*, Vol. 1.

42 Matthison's painting of Merton Tower with Corpus Christi Gateway (left) is from Peel and Minchin's *Oxford*. "Dahlia Amber", a photograph by Ernest Marriage printed from blocks by Arthur Cox for the Illustrating Co., was published in the 1903 *Process Year Book*; "Dahlias" (right) is from the 1913–14 edition of the same publication. The image of white willow flowers and leaves is from *Familiar Trees*.

43 Matthison's painting (left) of Queen's College Gateway is from *Oxford* by Peel and Minchin. The advertisement detail for Oxford Marmalade comes from *Near Oxford*.

44 The 1908 Frith postcard of the interior of Exeter College Chapel (bottom right) is from *The Oxford Explorer*. The view of Exeter College (bottom left) is from *Pictures in Colour of Oxford*.

45 The image of the Divinity School (bottom left) is from *100 Views of Oxford*. On the right is the Divinity School, painted by William Matthison for Peel and Minchin's *Oxford*. The photograph of the 1910 Encaenia Ceremony (top right) comes from *The Oxford Explorer*.

46 "The Barges" and "The Eights", painted by William Matthison, come from Peel and Minchin's *Oxford*. "The College Barges and Folly Bridge" was painted by E.W. Haslehurst for his *Cambridge*. The drawing by Lancelot Speed, "Waiting for the Cox" (bottom left), is from Lang's *Oxford*.

47 The main picture of the Sheldonian Theatre is from *Pictures in Colour of Oxford*. The small inset of the entrance gates to Clarendon and the Sheldonian, painted by William Matthison, comes from Peel and Minchin's *Oxford*.

48 The main picture of Jesus College comes from *Pictures in Colour of Oxford*. The Welsh dragon is from the cover of *Beautiful Wales* by Edward Thomas, another A&C Black *Twenty Shilling* title published in 1905.

49 The 1902 Frith postcard of Exeter College is from *The Oxford Explorer*. The illustration of the leaves and flower of the acacia comes from *Familiar Trees*, Vol. 3.

50 The 1914 view of Trinity College Lime Walk (bottom right) comes from *The Oxford Explorer*. Trinity Gate, painted by Yoshio Markino, is from Hugh de Sélincourt's *Oxford from Within*.

51 The 1911 Frith postcard of St Alban's Quad of Merton College (bottom left) is from *The Oxford Explorer*. The map of Merton College is from *Merton College, Oxford*. The sycamore leaves and flowers are from *Familiar Trees*, Vol. 1.

52 The main image of Oriel College is from *Pictures in Colour of Oxford*. The cover and illustration of an extension ladder are from *Thompson's Gardener's Assistant*, Vol. 1.

53 The 1912 Frith postcard of Magdalen College Deer Park (left) is from *The Oxford Explorer*. On the right is the same view in a painting by Matthison from Peel and Minchin's *Oxford*. "Snake's Head Fritillary" comes from *Flowers of the Field* by Rev. C.A. Johns, with illustrations by E.N. Gwatkin, published by Routledge in 1907. The flower of the common elm, on the left, is from *Familiar Trees*, Vol 1.

BIBLIOGRAPHY

54 The main image of New College is from *Pictures in Colour of Oxford*. In the middle is a detail from a hymn postcard published by Philco Co. in London, *c*.1910, and printed in Germany. The inset on the left, New College Cloisters, is a Matthison painting from Peel and Minchin's *Oxford*.

55 The photograph of Broad Street at the top was taken around 1920 and is from *The Oxford Explorer*. Broad Street, painted by Matthison (bottom right) is from Peel and Minchin's *Oxford*. The advertisements for bicycles and motor cars are from *Near Oxford*, published by Alden & Co. in 1904.

56 The painting of the High Street and Carfax (right) is from Peel and Minchin's *Oxford*. The interior of Oxford Town Hall, *c*. 1900 (left), is from *The Oxford Explorer*. The advertisement for Boffin's Restaurant comes from *Alden's Oxford Guide*.

57 On the left is E.W. Haslehust's painting of Magdalen College from the Cherwell, from his *Oxford*. The three varieties of *Cypripdeium* (centre inset) come from *Thompson's Gardener's Assistant*, Vol. 1, as does "Flower of the Cistus".

58 The map and cover are from *Up and Down the River: Bennet's Map and Guide to the Thames*, published in 1906.

59 The main image is a painting by E.W. Haslehust of Oxford from Headington Hill, from his *Oxford*. The view of Addison's Walk (left) is from *Pictures in Colour of Oxford*. The photograph (right) shows Headington Hill Hall.

60 The image of the Ashmolean Museum at the bottom is from *The Oxford Explorer*.

Adventurers All, Rita Ricketts, Blackwell, 1988.
All Souls in My Time, A.L. Rowse, Duckworth, 1993.
Exploring Oxford, Michael De-la-Noy, Headline, 1991.
History of the Bodleian Library, 1845–1945, Edmund Craster, Clarendon, 1952.
Near Oxford, H.T. Inman, Alden, 1913.
Oxford, Michael Hall, Pevensey Press, 1981.
Oxford, F.D. How, Blackie, 1915.
Oxford, Andrew Lang, Seeley, 1890.
Oxford, Jan Morris, OUP, 1965.
Oxford, Robert Peel and H.C. Minchin, Methuen, 1905.
Oxford, An Architectural Guide, Geoffrey Tyack, OUP, 1998.
Oxford and Cambridge, An Uncommon History, Peter Sager, Thames & Hudson, 2005.
Oxford and its Colleges, J. Wells, Methuen, 1923.
Oxford, As It Was and As It Is Today, Christopher Hobhouse, Batsford, 1939.
Oxford, A Sketchbook, Fred Richards, A&C Black, 1915.
Oxford from Within, Hugh de Sélincourt, Chatto & Windus, 1910.
Oxford, Images and Reflections, John Davison and Anna Howard, Blackwell, 1995.
Oxford Renowned, L. Rice-Oxley, Methuen, 1947.
Oxford Observed, Peter Snow, Murray, 1991.
Oxfordshire Within Living Memory, Countryside Books/ Oxfordshire Federation of Women's Institutes, 1994.
The Encyclopaedia of Oxford, Christopher and Edward Hibbert, 1988.
The Illustrated History of Oxford University, John Prest (ed.), OUP, 1993.
The University of Oxford Botanic Gardens, Louise Allen and Timothy Walker, University of Oxford Botanic Garden, 1995.

www.communigate.co.uk/oxford/holywellcemetery/index
www.headington.org.uk
www.bodley.ox.ac.uk
www.chch.ox.ac.uk
www.ox.ac.uk
www.oxfordcity.co.uk

The Times Past Archive

The *Memories of Times Past* series would be inconceivable without the massive Times Past Archive, a treasury of books, magazines, atlases, postcards and printed ephemera from the "golden age" of colour printing between 1895 and 1915.

From the time several years ago when the project was first conceived, the collecting of material from all over the world has proceeded in earnest. As well as a complete set of the 92 A&C Black 20 *Shilling* colour books, which are the inspiration for the series, the Archive houses full sets of period *Baedeker* and *Murray's Guides*, almost every colour-illustrated travel book from illustrious publishing houses like Dent, Jack, Cassell, Blackie and Chatto & Windus, and a massive collection of reference works with colour plates on subjects from railways and military uniforms to wild flowers and birds' eggs.

The Archive also contains complete runs of all the important periodicals of the time that contained colour illustrations, including the pioneering *Penrose's Pictorial Annual: An Illustrated Review of the Graphic Arts*; the first-ever British colour magazine, *Colour*; ladies' magazines like *Ladies' Field* and *The Crown*; and more popular titles like *The Connoisseur* and *The London Magazine*.

These years were vintage years for atlas publishing, and the Times Past Archive contains such gems as Keith Johnston's *Royal Atlas of Modern Geography*, *The Harmsworth Atlas*, Bartholomew's *Survey Atlas of England and Wales*, and the *Illustrated and Descriptive Atlas of The British Empire*.

Last but not least, the Archive includes a wealth of smaller items — souvenirs, postcards, tickets, programmes, catalogues, posters, and all the colourful ephemera with which the readers of the original 20 *Shilling* books would have been familiar.

The Times Past Website

The website to accompany this project can be found at www.memoriesoftimespast.com, where you will find further information about the birth and development of the project, together with the complete original texts of titles published to date. There is also an area where you can take part in discussions raised by readers of the books who want to take their interest further and share their memories and passions with others. The website will start small and elegant, as you would expect of an "Edwardian website", but it will gradually become what you and we together make it, a place for devotees of art and culture from a century ago to meet and be inspired.

Every effort has been made to ensure the accuracy of the information presented in this book. The publisher will not assume liability for damages caused by inaccuracies in the data and makes no warranty whatsoever expressed or implied. The publisher welcomes comments and corrections from readers, which will be incorporated in future editions. Please email corrections@memoriesoftimespast.com

Acknowledgements

Pat Alexander, Iffley
Ken Crozier, Kennington
The Centre for Oxfordshire Studies
Oxford Central Library
Janet Keene
Friends of Holywell Cemetery
Jonathan Smith
Julian Tester, The Book Lover
Glynn Waite, and the Transport History Collection at Brunel University, for images of period railway tickets.

Many of the early postcards and photographs included in this book have been collected by Hugo Brown on a CD, *The Oxford Explorer CD-ROM*. More information about this publication, together with ordering information, can be found at www.cambridge-explorer.org.uk/TOE.htm

Iffley Road, painted by Yoshio Markino, in *Oxford from Within* by Hugh de Sélincourt, Chatto & Windus, 1910.

Milton Fm
Upper Milton
Milton Field
Shipton und Willichw^d
Boyntn Copse
Shipton Downs
Potter's Hill
Leafield
Waterloo Fm
Fordwells
WYCHWOOD FOREST
Lit. Park
Fawler
Finstock
Wilcote
Manor Ho.
Combe
East End
Stonesfield
Slate Quarries
Littleworth Fm
BLENHEIM PARK
Old Bletchington
WOODSTOCK
Hensington Ho.
Shipton on Cherwell
Blenheim Palace
Bladon
Kidlington
Round Cas.

Fulbrook
White Oak G^n
Dell End
North Leigh
East End
Ch. Handborough
Long Handbor.
Handboro'
Brooks Mill
Begbrook
Burleigh Fm
Yarnton

Swinbrook
Asthall Leigh
Haley
Hailey Com
Eynsham Hall
Eynsham Camp
Freeland
Purwell Fm
Yarnton Yarnton
Worton

Widford
Manor F.
AKEMAN ST.
Minster Lovell
Crawley
Withridge Cross
Coggs Copse
Eynsham Park
Little Green Fm
Howling Cross
Paper Mill
Isis River
Cassington

Asthall
Windrush Riv.
Curbridge
Downs Fm
WITNEY
Northfield
Hailey
Hill Ho.
Clements Fields
Twelve Acre Fm
Eynsham
Wytham

Signett
Asthall Barrow
Starveall Fm
Witney Park Fm
Coggs
High Coggs
Sth Leigh
Chelmore
S. Leigh
Pinkhill Fm
Swinford
Botley
Wytham Park
Woodend Fm

Shilton
Grove Fm
Charterville Allotments
Astrop Fm
Emmas Ditch
Witney
Rectory Mill
Mill
Tor Wood
Sutton
Farmoor
Hilleind Fm

Norton Pits
Manor Ho.
Curbridge Com
Duckling ton
Hill Houses
Hardwick
Stanton Harcourt
Skinners Weir
West End Leys Fm
Chawley Fm
Wink

Broadwell Gr
Alvescott Downs Fm
Norton Brize
Barrow
Grove
Lew
Lew Heath
Cokethorpe
Home W^d
The Devils Quoit
Underdown Mill
Eaton H^th
Eaton
Gumner
Bradley Wm

Kencott
Shill Fm
Marsh Hadden
Claywell Fm
Yelford
Old Farm
Northmoor
Lt. Bradly

Alvescott
Black Bourton
Aston Sheep Com
New Shifford Fm
Brighthampton
Standlake
Radwell Fm
Appleton
Tubney Fm

Broadwell
Rooks Hill
BAMPTON in the Bush
Bates Land
Aston
Aston Com^n
Cote
Aston Low^r. Com.
Shifford
Com^n
Moorton
Newbridge
Appleton
Bessilsleigh Com
Sandford
Wood

Clanfield
Lit. Clanfield
Weald
Quackerham Ford
Chimney
Thames side Fm
Duxford
Longworth
Fyfield
Frilford
Tubney War.
Cothill

Grafton
Barns
Charney Br.
Radcot Gr
Tadpole
Lower Newton
Hinton Waldrist
Welmore
Longworth Ho.
Frilford Heath
Oakley Ho.
Frilford
Sheepstead Fm
Shippon Com.

Kelmscot
R. Isis or Thames
Buckland
Kingstone
Bagpuze
Fyfield Wick
Marcham
ABINGDON

Faringdon Pk.
Pusey Ho.
Charbury Camp
Pusey
Garford
Noahs Ark
R. Ock
Drayton Field
Drayton
Kennist

Coxwell
E
FARINGDON
Hatford
Charney Basset
Lyford
Wilts Canal
East Hanney Field
Steventon Field

Park
Little Coxwell
Stanford in the Vale
West Hanney
East Hanney
Berks Canal
Barn
Steventon
Mill

Beckett Park
Longcot
Uffington
Goosey
Challow
Denchworth
Wantage
West Hendred
Steventon